Religious Integrity for Everyone

Functional Theology for Secular Society

Rev. Fred Campbell

Writers Club Press

San Jose · New York · Lincoln · Shanghai

Religious Integrity for Everyone
Functional Theology for Secular Society

Copyright © 2000 Fred Campbell

ISBN: 0-595-00038-X

Published by Writers Club Press, an imprint of iUniverse.com, Inc.

For information address:
iUniverse.com, Inc.
620 North 48th Street
Suite 201
Lincoln, NE 68504-3467
www.iuniverse.com

URL: http://www.writersclub.com

Campbell, Fred F.
Ix, 165 p.
1. Liberalism (Religion)
2. Language and languages-English-Religious aspects
3. Secularization (Theology)-Encyclopedias and dictionaries I. Title II.s
Campbell, Fred F. BL31.C2 1999
1. Religion-Dictionaries
2. Faith-20th century
3. English language-Dictionaries I. Title II Campbell, Fred F.
200.3014 C2 1999

Contents

Preface

I have just completed 31 years of ministry with congregations whose members were deeply embedded in secular culture. This is to recognize that values drawn from the sciences, technology, democracy, and capitalism informed how these members understood living and interacting with the reality of society and nature. In America Christianity has been the dominant religion and Judaism has been a constant minority presence. Only in very large cities has there been evidence of other major religions. This is an essay about the tension between individuals seeking to live with integrity in a cultural setting in which secular and Christian ideas are in dramatic tension. Although some will respond to my essay as if it were an attack on Christianity, this is not my intent. I believe it describes the cultural reality in which Christianity now works to maintain a vital presence.

During this 30-year time period, secular culture grew into an equal, if not a stronger, source of knowledge about living than Christianity. Before World War II, Christianity was the primary religion in America, informing people about the meaning of life and the values that led to the good life. Now TV, our public schools, and universities—the institutions of secular culture—have so grown in influence that they dominate as our source of knowing. In some cases it is not so much that they give people a way of knowing the meaning of living as that they consume our work and play time.

All religious language and practice, during this same period, have been removed from our American public realm in the name of separation of church and state. Christian prayer, symbols, and Bible readings are no longer part of many public gatherings. This separation of Christianity and secular culture has progressed to the extent that children growing up after 1985 may very well reach maturity without any formal or direct knowledge or experience of Christianity or any other religion.

While my ministry immersed me among people who were deeply involved in secular culture, I certainly continued to recognize the dominant role that Christianity played in our culture over the last 500 years. As a consequence, every word in English having to do with religious ideas depends upon Christian theology. One cannot easily think or speak of theological concerns outside of a Christian context. In effect, the link between Christianity and religion within the English language is so close that "religion" seems to mean Christianity, particularly in the United States. This presents a challenge to people who live within secular culture and who have religious concerns outside the boundaries of Christianity. Anyone speaking and thinking in English who has a religious concern or idea and does not wish to express it in words tainted with Christian meaning has a problem. How can we think and speak when there are no words to articulate our ideas?

Three possible responses to this situation occur to me:
1.   Forget the whole matter. Give up on being religious in secular culture.
2.   Create a new vocabulary.
3.   Stretch or modify the accepted meaning of words to cover the relationship between their traditional and new meanings.

This book presents how I developed the third option.

Religious concerns have always bothered me. I have been unable to either forget them or set them aside. I believe that human health depends upon vital and vibrant religious faith and hope. The health of individuals and human communities depends on integrity of religious understanding and practice. To create a new vocabulary to achieve this end is like introducing a foreign language to deal with something personal and intimate that is of vital importance. This option just does not work. So I propose functional definitions for established religious words. Christianity becomes an example of their meanings, not the only possible illustration.

These practical definitions emerged over several years as I was struggling to respond to another challenge. Within my congregations some individuals lived within a secular world view and carried an understanding of Christianity they had learned as children. Not only did this religious perspective leave them with emotional scars, it no longer made any sense. Because it was the only meaning of Christianity they knew, they rejected most religious ideas expressed in traditional words. These individuals knew what they did not believe, but had very little idea of what they did believe.

Another group of congregants I served had never been in any church or religious community. Their ideas of religion came from what they had heard on the radio or TV. These folks were and are struggling to find out what religion is all about. They know they need a source of meaning in their lives and a community to validate their personal identity, values, and ways of understanding life and being human. Religion is somehow expected to fulfill these needs.

My liberal religious tradition claims to meet this two-fold challenge without a single defining creed or set of dogmas. It invites every generation to respond with reason to the events of life and come together in community to celebrate religious meaning, faith, and hope. As I worked within this environment, I gradually realized that I was hearing the English language used to express four different faith perspectives: humanism, naturalism, mysticism, and theism.

People using each of the four faiths reach into their surrounding reality for a source of meaning and values that, in every case, is larger than or transcendent of the individual. I have come to call these sources of meaning and value *transcendent reference systems* because individuals use them as the authority for how they live their lives.

As a minister serving people who lived within secular culture, as I also did, I sought to bring religious meaning and faith as a response to the crises and celebrations of living. Individuals need to know the meaning of the events of death, loss, depression, doubt, anxiety, and grief. They want to place births, weddings, anniversaries, and the triumphs of their struggles within a context larger than a passing moment soon to be forgotten. When I realized that functional religious language allowed me to express the four faiths and would enable me to separate clearly the issues with which each faith struggled, my ministry gained depth. It became both more fulfilling to me and more beneficial to those I served.

As I worked to gain clarity for the ideas presented here I was informed by the published lectures of Alfred North Whitehead. So I want to acknowledge a long-standing debt to him for quickening my insights into religion and for broadening my understanding of our ways of human knowing. Specifically I have drawn upon his little book *Religion in the Making* and modified his definitions of religion given there. I also use his definitions of empirical and rational from the opening sections of *Process and Reality* to shape my thoughts. Although I first read his works many years ago, the ideas of organism and process now haunt and inform my thinking in more ways than I can say.

Next I need to recognize Barb Marquardt who pushed me to fully develop "The Four Faiths" as an adult religious education course. I thank members of the congregations I served in Indianapolis, Indiana; Rochester, Minnesota; Fort Collins, Colorado; northwest Atlanta, Georgia; Schenectady, New York; St. Louis, Missouri; Kalamazoo, Michigan; and Lincoln, Nebraska, for being participants as I presented and developed the ideas which follow in subsequent chapters. In Lincoln, Jim Kimberly encouraged me to write an actual manuscript; no, it is more accurate to report that he demanded I do it because these ideas had resolved questions he had been worrying about for many years. Thank you, Jim. I am also deeply appreciative of the two women who read and gave me editorial input that brought polish to the manuscript Jim demanded, Eva Hochgarf and Diane Worden.

I believe the insights which follow name a primary challenge that is confronting traditional Christianity. Fundamentalists and evangelicals probably will be very uncomfortable with my placement of Christianity as just one of many religious options in our larger culture. However, I think that some Christians may find that using the four faiths will bring renewed vitality to their confession. They may also use the functional language of religion suggested here as a way to reach people who are so deeply involved in secular culture that they do not hear the Christian message.

This book presents the functional definitions I worked out in the service of the four faiths. Perhaps I should say, this book presents the functional religious language I suggest as a response to our human need for vital and vibrant religion within secular culture.

Fred F. Campbell
October 1999

Chapter 1

The Crisis of Religious Integrity

I believe a crisis of religious integrity in American-European culture is spreading under the influence of secularism. The secular understanding of our world, based on science and technology, has been and continues to be very successful in manipulating the material aspects of our human environment. It has given us the power of flight, of curing illness, of rapid travel, of weather prediction, of warm houses in winter and cool ones in summer, of a food supply in vast variety and quantity. It dominates our educational institutions. And now that the paradigm of the sciences dominates our living and thinking, religion is suffering a crisis of integrity.

This crisis actually affects all of the world's religions. Most religions claim to offer the only way to spiritual health and order for individual and community life. When followers of one religion live next to followers of another, this claim is implicitly challenged. This challenge is intensified as followers of the established world religions redistribute themselves throughout the globe and confront each other. They now live in communities within cities and nations that include people with religions different than their own. All of us live within culture that is increasingly secular, a fact not as true just 25 years ago.

What is Integrity?

My *American Heritage Dictionary* defines integrity as "a state of being unimpaired, whole, complete." I use **integrity** throughout this book to refer to the relationship between human experience and the words used to describe that experience. A person has integrity when his or her words communicate congruence with personal experience and the experiences of other people. People have integrity when they say what they mean and do what they say. Their words describe reality as others remember it and experience it. This is what it means to tell the truth. I hear the truth when someone else puts into words what I have experienced, or may experience, in the world in which we both live.

I have a friend who tells good stories about the events of her living. However, she tends to make the stories more impressive by exaggerating the details. To hear her story of an event in which I have participated forces me to wonder what happened to the reality I remember. From my point of view, she lacks integrity. I never know what is "true" and what has been dramatized for effect. Because I like her nevertheless, I have come to accept her exaggerated stories as part of who she is.

Integrity is a more serious problem when our leaders lack it. They have the power to govern and shape the world we must live in. Politicians create a problem of credibility, implying a lack of personal integrity, when they promise on the campaign trail to do things the voters know can't be done or promise not to do something that once in office they find they should now do. For example, President George Bush said, "No new taxes!" and then found himself amid circumstances that dictated the wise thing to do was to raise taxes. And Ronald Reagan promised that if he were elected, he would not raise taxes, would increase military spending, and would reduce the national deficit. He found he could not do all three. In fact, he did only one—raise military spending.

President Bill Clinton's problem of integrity rests on the numerous meanings of the word "sex" in the English language. All agree his relationship with Monica Lewinski developed into something inappropriate because of its sexual aspects. He admitted as much. His situation is complicated by people who did not like him for other reasons and used this opportunity to humiliate him in hopes of diminishing his power. Also, the fuzzy line between what should be private, as opposed to public, in a person's life is not well established in our society. Having considered all this, the American people were left with troubling questions. Can we believe what Clinton says on other topics? How isolated is this inappropriate behavior in his life? These are questions of integrity.

People have credibility problems when they say things about the world we share that do not correspond with what we have experienced or what we believe about our world. Lying violates integrity directly, but a person with a credibility problem is one who is merely suspected of lacking integrity. Telling the truth about the world in which we live or about our human living marks a person with integrity.

What is Religious Integrity?

Religions intend to bring spiritual health to human lives. Yet, in today's world, many people find religious language and participation irrelevant. This discrepancy between religious intent and what is happening in the actual world highlights the problem of religious integrity.

A religion has integrity when it enables human beings to enact the drama of living, aging, and dying with understanding and acceptance, meaning and purpose, trust and love, faith and hope. A religion has integrity when its articulated understandings about our world and our living "make sense." A religion suffers a crisis of integrity only when its spoken truths and practices no longer meet the needs of the people it seeks to serve.

Where and How Is It Missing?

I believe this crisis of religious integrity manifests itself at both the institutional and personal levels. How is religious integrity missing in our society? The symptoms of this crisis at the institutional level are many, and all of them attest to the crisis of religious integrity to which I am pointing:

- Churches of many European countries are empty.
- Membership of many Protestant main line congregations has been declining over the last few years.
- A division is growing between a combination of evangelical and fundamentalist Christians and other Christians.
- What it means to be a Baptist is splitting the Southern Baptist Church.
- Some Christian groups react defensively in society, based on a perceived threat to their standing and integrity.
- Fewer men and women are entering religious vocations within the Roman Catholic Church than ever before.
- The separation of church and state controversy within the United States has at its core the questions of what is religion and its worth in society.
- Large numbers of people in their twenties and thirties have little or no firsthand experience and knowledge of religion.

People experience a crisis of religious integrity when any or all of the following things happen:

- Their religion cannot answer a question of meaning for which they must have an answer.
- Explanations given by their religious faith for an experience, such as the death of a child, are unacceptable and unworkable. Working though grief is difficult, if not impossible.
- They realize that life's meaning escapes them.
- Their religion does not work or make sense as they confront the reality of the world in which they live.

- Engaging in religious ritual one day a week does not connect or influence living during the other six days.
- The apparent wide distance between religion and science leaves them pondering.
- When a Christian implies that only Christians can be good people, they feel uncomfortable. Religion on the defensive within our secular society arouses discomfort.

Are you lacking religious integrity? If you have ever attended a religious worship service with a congregation of your choice and found yourself unable to say or believe some of the words of a creed or sing some words of a hymn, then you have experienced this crisis. If you have had silent reservations about some parts of the service, then you know the tension existing at the root of religion's crisis of integrity. When worship does not deal with the world as you know it or fails to add meaning to your life, then that religion conducting such worship has a problem of integrity. Either it must change the meaning of the words it uses or you must do the work to connect them with the world as you know it.

If you have come to believe that neither Christianity nor other religions speak to the events and concerns of your living, then you are suffering from this crisis of religious integrity. If it seems to you that religion is dealing with, speaking about, a world about which you know nothing or very little, then there is a distance between the reality of your life and the language religion is using. This is a problem of integrity for religion because religion intends to add meaning to human living, not confusion.

If you are a minister with a different understanding of faith than your parish members have, you are caught in the heart of this integrity crisis. Particularly if you fear that to share honestly what you believe and understand will cost you your job or your status of Reverend in your denomination, you are then living this crisis of integrity.

In southwestern Michigan a few years ago, a minister of a conservative Christian church said in public that he accepted other ways to be

Christian than his particular faith calling. He also welcomed gays into his congregation. In order to maintain the integrity of their church, a group of ministers in his denomination charged him with heresy. No matter that he was convicted; his congregation valued him so much that they voted to support and follow him out of the denomination. This is a clear example of institutional and personal integrity clashing.

Tension and Integrity

Tension exists between persons of faith who claim that theirs is the only valid religion and the American belief in acceptance of numerous particular religions as valid. This axiom of American society states that religious differences will not be allowed to disrupt the public realm we all share and enjoy. There is a point at which these two beliefs are in conflict and create a problem for personal integrity. Many people who affirm both seem not to feel the tension. However, I predict that this symptom will disturb the peace of mind of more people. As the diversity of religions increases in our cities and becomes more obvious, claims of exclusive religious identity will be more difficult to maintain.

As individuals, people are choosing not to participate in or support religious institutions. This drift away from a public commitment occurs because institutional words and rituals do not give meaning to their lives. Or, is it that they find so much to do in the secular world that they have no time left to join in religious activities? In each case, the connection between religion and living is so vague and weak that individuals decide to block out formal religion from their lives. To meet this need for connection, many churches in America have expanded the range of activities they offer way beyond what has been considered traditional.

Have you ever been to a funeral and felt that the service did not meet your needs to grieve and affirm the meaning of living? When mourners in attendance at a funeral service sense an inadequate faith response to death, they experience the tension that is at the heart of this religious crisis of integrity as they leave the service. Funerals and memorial services which do not meet the needs of the living—first to grieve and then move on to an affirmation of faith—fail badly and show that religion has a problem with integrity.

Two possible understandings may inform your "funeral disconnect" experience:

1. *The service was within the tradition you participate in on a regular basis.* However, the actuality of the service did not deal with the reality of the life that is over or with the circumstances of the death or with the feelings and thoughts of the survivors in attendance. Or maybe it ended with a statement of faith and hope that seemed to be an inadequate response. You leave facing the prospect of living with this loss and with your fresh knowledge of death as part of living without an affirmation of faith that enables you to go on in spite of this grief.

2. *Your deceased friend was a member of a different religion from yours.* You are Christian and your friend was Buddhist, for example. These two religions speak different languages derived from very different understandings of life's meaning. You and your friend shared no common understanding of religion. In some cases, even the various sects of Christianity are so far apart that the rituals and language of one will not meet the needs and expectations of a Christian from another sect. You leave the service without having met your needs to grieve and renew your faith.

The failure of the service to meet your needs is basically a language problem. In English no understanding of religion's function includes all the various ways we humans are religious. In our world there are many long-established ways to practice religion. Each is somewhat isolated from the others, but now all attempt to use English to fulfill their function in individual lives. Or, is it that many of us alive today, who depend on English to express religious concerns, have no language to articulate our ideas of what life means to us? What we need is a way to understand and connect our various ways of being religious. We need a set of words that enables us to easily translate from one religious tradition to another.

Fifty years or more ago the religions of our world were relatively isolated. From the Euro-American point of view, Buddhism and Hinduism were in Asia, Shintoism in Japan, Islam in the Arab world, and Christianity in its many forms dominated Europe and the Americas. Each one claimed the Truth, with a capital T, in its own way and to be the only one to have it. Christianity makes this claim when it says that God sent His *only* Son to save humanity. Islam implies this when saying, "There is only one God, Allah." Judaism also implies the same with its claim to be *the* Chosen People who are participants in a *unique* covenant with the one God.

These claims have gone unchallenged since most people have experienced only one way to be religious and, therefore, human. To be human is to be religious. Americans have always lived with the tension created by the variety of Christian churches in proximity to the three traditions within Judaism. Now, with travel and communication links all over the world, religious diversity is growing in every country. It is increasingly difficult to be a follower of one religion and not know of others. Maintaining isolation within one religious tradition is almost impossible when meeting or having social or economic interchange with people adhering to another religion. The claims of having the only truth about how to be human no longer stand unchallenged.

At the individual level, the many ways to seek and sustain spiritual health contribute to each religion's crisis of integrity. Now the challenge to all peoples and nations is finding how to live peacefully in one world, in each nation, in every city, all of which contain ethnic, religious, and racial diversity.

How will the kind of violence between the Protestants and Catholics of Northern Ireland over the last 30 years be avoided in the future? How may peace overcome the fear, hatred, and violence between Muslim and Hindu in India and Pakistan? How will the economic integration of Europe be accomplished without civil unrest? How will the tribal animosities of Africa be kept from war? How will the religious tensions in the United States be kept from justifying bombings and killings over issues such as abortion and religious integrity?

Diversity of religion contributes to the problems each religious community has in maintaining its integrity. In the United States, we Americans seem to agree, with some exceptions, that we will not allow religious differences to draw us into violent conflict. We will accept differences in religious faith and practice and not allow these to disrupt the public realms of politics, economics, education, and social intercourse. This acceptance of religious diversity is an ongoing challenge to the claims of absolute truth made by most religions. It bears witness to the many ways human beings may live spiritually healthy lives.

Another dimension of this crisis of integrity in religion, both at the individual and the community level, may be found in every country where past religious traditions and modern secular culture clash. I believe consequences grow out of the increasing influence and dominance of technology as a source of knowledge and lifestyle in our world.

Redefining the Language of Religion

I will suggest in what follows that another major contributing factor to this crisis, which threatens the peace and meaning of life, is that religious words in the English language are formally defined in terms of Christianity. All the words expressing religious ideas and concerns in English carry a prejudice for Christianity. No applicable words in English adequately express the religious concerns, faith, hope, and ideas of people who are neither Christian nor comfortable with conservative Christian theology.

Although I am not a linguist, I suspect that every language is tied to some religious perspective in the same way. Therefore, I have accepted the task of presenting a set of functional word meanings that include Christianity and enable any other religious perspective to express its religious faith and concerns with integrity. The purpose of my extensive essay in creative theology is to propose such a set of functional definitions for key words in English. I believe that these functional definitions are needed to express religious ideas and faith. They are universal enough to maintain integrity in everyone who gives expression to religion in their living. There are three aspects to my proposal:

1.   *A set of functional definitions for religious words and ideas*—Each sect of Christianity, each of the world's religions, becomes an example of these definitions and not the only possible religious option open to human beings.

2.   *Religion as transcendent reference systems of meaning*— Six of the universal concerns of religion, which follow from an individual's engagement with the transcendent, will be defined, discussed, and developed in some detail.

3.   *Four faiths within secular culture*—Based on my experience, there are four viable faiths. Each is defined by how language is used. Through each one of them, individuals may find spiritual health. Specifically, they are Humanism, Naturalism, Mysticism, and Theism.

Throughout my ministerial career I have struggled to make sense of the many voices I have heard that were reaching for meaning in the routine process of living. Now I understand that every individual reaches out beyond the self into patterns of relationships to draw a personal set of values upon which his or her life's meaning depends. Over the years it dawned on me that I was hearing four distinct ways to use English. Each was expressing a different faith that drew its values from a transcendent reference:

- **Humanists** find life's meaning within the human community—past, present, and future;
- **Naturalists** understand that humans are part of the natural world and draw their meaning of living from this context;
- **Mystics** have had an experience of "union with some transcendent whole," an experience so powerful that it shapes their values;
- **Theists** know that God exists, and their values derive from this knowledge and relationship.

In a sense, all of the ideas mentioned above are interdependent, so they will not necessarily be presented in the order used above. I will use **bold type** for each word to introduce its functional definition.

Chapter 2

Religious Integrity Depends on Language

Integrity, in the way I am using this word, has to do with the link between human experiences and the words used to refer to them. One of the little-noticed aspects of this crisis is that the language of religion no longer seems adequate and applicable to the way many human beings experience living in American and European cultures. Religious words, as defined in English-language dictionaries and as used in popular culture, no longer connect with real-life experiences of many men and women. These religious words, when used by religious leaders called clergy, are puzzling and incomprehensible to many in our culture. Consequently, participation in formal religion is declining because it seems irrelevant to life lived in today's secular culture as it moves toward and beyond the year 2000.

One of the reasons people are finding religious language irrelevant and inapplicable to our world is that in America, at least, it has been largely removed from public education. From 1970 to 1995 religious language, symbols, and rituals were excised from secular education and public practice. Their removal has meant the disappearance of Christian symbols and practice from school routine and public meeting spaces in the name of separation of church and state. That many Christians feel threatened as a consequence should not surprise anyone. As another result, secular education has become dominated by the values and perspective derived from the sciences. While many children growing up during this time did not receive any education in the use of religious language or ideas, many adults experienced much less religious language in the public realm of social discourse than they did in their own childhood. Those youth who obtain their education from religion-sponsored schools are notable exceptions.

Because all aspects of religion (in most cases, Christianity particularly) have been excluded from the public secular realm of society, people in current secular culture do not have a shared understanding of religion. Instead of a generic religion, there are only specific religious systems, such as Roman Catholic, Lutheran, and Baptist perspectives within Christianity; and Unitarian Universalism, Judaism, Islam, Hinduism outside of it. There is no overall definition or understanding of religion that covers all of these specific ways of practicing religion.

In contrast, many specific sciences are part of an overarching structure of Science. Each discipline claims a broadly understood subject area and uses the scientific method to gain knowledge about it. Particular sciences narrow the ability to predict results or consequences and extend the power to control events in our world. This allows people who specialize in one branch of science to understand, talk to, and respect people in all other branches.

Religion has no such common structure. If one isolates himself within a community that has only one religion, few problems occur unless and until that religion cannot deal with the more dramatic events of human living. However, in every religiously diverse city and nation, where no common overarching understanding of religion exists, people in their own faith tradition have no basis for understanding and respecting the faiths of others. This book seeks to set forth the needed general understanding of religion which we have lacked up to now.

When faced with a religious word whose meaning is unknown, an English-language dictionary will be of limited value. All religious words, and therefore all religious ideas, are defined there in terms of Christian theology, a somewhat narrow range of possibilities. Meanings frequently seem so far from what the individual may have experienced that it is irrelevant and inapplicable to today's world. The definitions are not applicable to religious experience other than Christian. Even some liberal Christians are uncomfortable with dictionary definitions.

This is the premise upon which this book begins, let me say again. All definitions found in dictionaries of the English language are given as if Christianity were the only religious perspective open to human beings. If you want to discuss religion in English, you must either accept this Christian way of religion or redefine the words or work around the dictionary meanings in some way. Religious diversity is becoming a fact of life as our cities and towns increasingly include practitioners of many faiths. As our acceptance of religious diversity grows to include world religions other than Christianity, we face difficult semantic barriers in discussing religious concerns shared by the different religions. If one comes to religious concerns from within the secular world, there seems to be no way to be religious. If one lives within the worldview of nature presented by the sciences, religion may seem precluded because dictionaries define religion as depending upon a belief in or knowledge of a supernatural being, God.

Let me illustrate. In my third edition of *The American Heritage Dictionary of the English Language*, religion is defined in this way:

1.a. Belief in and reverence for a supernatural power or powers regarded as creator and governor of the universe.

b. A personal or institutionalized system grounded in such a belief and worship.

2. The life or condition of a person in a religious order.

3. A set of beliefs, values and practices based on the teachings of a spiritual leader.

4. A cause, a principle, or an activity pursued with zeal or conscientious devotion. Idiom: get religion.
    Informal: to accept a higher power as a controlling influence for the good in one's life.

I find these four meanings of religion unsatisfactory. I trust you also feel some discomfort because you may have had some religious experience that these definitions do not cover.

Note that the first definition restricts religion to "belief in and reverence for a supernatural power or powers." This is the primary meaning of religion in English usage. It implies that you are not religious if your understanding of God does not include the supernatural. The difficulty with this definition is that many people living and breathing today do not know what the supernatural is. They have never known if or when they may have experienced it. If you have never experienced the supernatural, then obviously you cannot be religious.

Let me purposely paraphrase this with its exclusionary intent: if you understand your experience of God to be within the natural realm of human experience, then you cannot have a religion or be religious or participate in religion. If your understanding of our universe and human living comes from within the scientific paradigm, you cannot have a religion because the paradigm that informs you deals with what is natural and denies existence to the supernatural. Your belief in a natural world that includes human beings and all that they may know appears left out of what the dictionary asserts as true.

Many Christians know and describe God as a natural phenomenon of our world. For many Christians and Jews and followers of other religions, the supernatural is not an operable category of experience or understanding.

In the previous two paragraphs I have assumed that the phrase "supernatural power or powers" refers to God which my dictionary tells me means the following:

    1.a.   A being conceived as the perfect, omnipotent, omniscient originator and ruler of the universe, the principal object of faith and worship in monotheistic religions.

       b.   The force, effect, or a manifestation or aspect of this being.

   c.   Christian Science: "Infinite mind; Spirit; Soul;
        Principle; Life; Truth; Love" (Mary Baker Eddy).
  2.   A being of supernatural powers or attributes believed
       in and worshipped by a people, especially a male
       deity thought to control some part of nature or reality.
  3.   An image of a supernatural being; an idol.
  4.   One that is worshipped, idolized, or followed:
       money was their god.

The concept of supernatural is integral to the understanding of God presented here. Connecting God with masculinity is an additional problem that today will give many discomfort, if not render the word unusable. Also, the three attributes of God (listed as perfect, omniscient, and omnipotent) are drawn from a narrow range of theological reflection. Many theologians conclude it is erroneous, if not unrealistic, to attribute these characteristics to God. More than a few understandings of God do not include them.

I suggest that experience of the supernatural is *one* way to God. It is not the only way. As human beings, we may know God and never leave or go outside of the natural realm that is our universe. What meaning might the word "God" have, if we accept that supernatural is not the only defining attribute of deity?

I recognize that many people believe in God but do not attribute the characteristics of perfection, omnipotence, and omniscience to that being (as some traditional Christians and others do) or describe God as the originator and ruler of the universe. More liberal Christians understand these four descriptions as coming from tradition and history, meeting the needs of theological questions in particular centuries past. Numerous challenges and questions have been raised about their appropriateness and helpfulness to our understanding of God in the twentieth and twenty-first centuries.

Buddhism and Hinduism are two great world religions in which there is no such God, while there were many gods in the religions of ancient Rome and Greece. For many Christians, much religious language is metaphor and poetry. These Christians live and think of their religion as carrying truth and meaning completely within a natural world.

My point is that religious words in our dictionaries assume the supernatural as a foundation of religion and are only relevant to a narrow range of Christianity today. These definitions come from past centuries. They are no longer adequate or applicable to the dominant worldview. They do not connect our experience to religious words and ideas and, therefore, contribute to the crisis of religious integrity in secular culture. This crisis cannot be ignored today.

If you are not convinced by my use of just two examples of religious words tied to Christianity, I invite you to pick up a dictionary and look up other religious words of your own choosing. Ask yourself if their definitions comfortably apply to all world religions. My answer is they do not. Next ask yourself if they help you express your experience of religion. Do these definitions help you say exactly what you mean? Again, I believe they do not, in many cases. I find dictionary definitions based on Christianity inadequate and inapplicable to expression of what I know about people's experience and religion.

I am interested in developing a set of definitions that enables us to understand religion as applicable to both those from within the natural world and those based on knowing the supernatural. The latter are real and vital to so many of the world's peoples that they must be considered viable options. Other viable options also exist, so let's look to them for additional understandings of religion.

New Definitions

For many years I listened to people living around me struggle to cope and deal with the religious concerns of their living. After reflecting upon their struggles, I have developed a set of functional definitions for religious words. I based them on the way religion functions in human experience and not on the content of Christianity.

If my definitions work, if they are helpful, every branch of Christianity will become an example instead of the only possibility under them. If they have power, they should help Christian clergy meet the needs of their congregants as well as reach out to people in the wider society. If they are relevant to today's world of religious diversity, they will enable people of differing religious faiths to converse about the same human problems and concerns. If they are broad enough and yet specific enough, they will enable us to understand how secular people may be religious. And they will give us a common language that enables the religions of our world to talk with each other about shared concerns central to our human condition. If they have validity, they will connect our experience with what we know and feel, thereby giving us words and concepts with which to be religious.

These functional definitions* will give us a means to resolve the crisis of religious integrity. They will give us words that connect with experience. They are what we need to enable us to think and act with religious integrity.

*A Footnote or Digression

Popular usage and the formal definitions in dictionaries do not always agree. Religious words as used by the news media are heavily influenced by secular culture. For example, the word "myth" to journalists means a story or belief that is false. However, in religion "myth" means a story seeking and intending to reveal meaning and insight about human living. As understood by religious persons, myths express important relationships between human beings and the world in which they live. It is only a small jump to realize that myths are to religion as theories are to science. Both seek to state relationships of interest, giving humans knowledge and understanding of their world.

Theories use the language of materialism. They tend to be constrained to objects and objective relationships. Their words have a literal, concrete referent. Myths frequently use words and elements of the story as symbols presenting a metaphor so that some words have multiple layers of meaning. One must stay aware of this and choose one or more levels of meaning which are of interest. Myths are about human life, past and present. The reality of human living is that much of it carries several levels of meaning and significance. Myths reflect this complex reality.

Chapter 3

Fundamental Definitions

Let us begin with a word that has always been essential to understanding religion, how people are religious, and what any religion may do for people. I believe it is generally understood that one of religion's main functions is to provide MEANING for the lives of individuals as well as communities of people. What is the meaning of meaning?

Take time to reflect on this question. Again, my dictionary is not much help. It defines meaning in terms of content:

1. Something that is conveyed or signified; sense or significance.
2. Something that one wishes to convey, especially by language: the writer's meaning was obscured by his convoluted prose.
3. An interpreted goal, intent, or end....

Years ago I first asked myself, "What is the meaning of meaning?" I was at camp as a minister to youth, watching and participating in a week of building community. I realized that the youth were having a very meaningful experience, yet I wondered, "Can there ever be a non-meaningful experience?" My answer then was that all human experience has some meaning. We may not like it, but there it is. Many experiences increase our understanding of life and our appreciation of life's meaning. I think that some experiences meet our expectations for meaning and significance, others do not. Some seem chaotic or disorienting and we say, "That was a meaningless experience."

After reaching these conclusions I suggest that **meaning** has to do with an increase or decrease of relatedness experienced by human beings to each other and to the elements of the reality which surrounds their lives. Relatedness is understood to have both quantity and quality as essential parameters.

Relatedness may have any or all of the following aspects: physical, emotional, mental, social, spiritual. Human relatedness comes in many different forms. When the meaning of living increases for us we gain insight, understanding, knowledge, friendship, perceived closeness, acceptance, connection, love, faith, hope. When meaning decreases in our living we feel let down, disappointed, disconnected, divorced, alienated, depressed, grief. Each of the preceding lists is meant to be suggestive, not exhaustive.

At the broadest level all education intends to increase the meaning in the lives of students and teachers. Formal education usually has factual knowledge as its primary subject. Facts about our physical world are one dimension of meaning. The way facts are related to each other and the surrounding reality is another.

Language is essential to honoring the meaning of our living. Because language enables us to name, reason, reflect, remember, imagine, and think, it is our primary means of communicating, ordering, and organizing. Language connects our concrete experiences with our world of mental activity. It is through the use of language that we clarify and intensify our understanding, interaction, and interdependence with all that surrounds us. All these activities contribute to increasing meaning in our lives. Without language there would be no meaning, only physical relationships; meaning is expressed through the use of language. Increasing the vitality and vibrancy of the meaning religion delivers to the lives of individuals is the intended purpose and value of this book.

When meaning is used in a religious context I think it has to do with the relationships individuals have with their surrounding communities and the ongoing process of change in our world. All useful work gives meaning to living. All human activities sustain and have meaning for those who participate. Religion's main task is to establish and sustain a special kind of meaning in the lives of human beings.

To separate religion from all other meaningful human activities, let me say that **religion** is what individuals and communities of individuals do with individual solitariness. I derived this definition from Alfred North Whitehead's original formulation in his little book *Religion in the Making.* His point was that each individual lives in solitariness and has to live his or her own life one day at a time. He then observed that when we humans are religious, we deepen, enrich, and integrate our experience and understanding of Self, Community, and God.

In our real secular world, the use of the word "God" has little or no meaning for many people. They do not know how it relates to their own experience. Either they have not had any experiences that lead to God or they do not have the language to name and reflect upon these experiences. How can they know what is being talked about? If religion is dependent upon God, and God is the supernatural as defined in the dictionary, then these people cannot be religious or participate in religion.

Let me substitute *transcendence* for Whitehead's God and allow God to be one form of transcendence. Now I may observe that religious meaning always includes at least three levels of human living: self, community, and transcendence. It is every religion's function to expand and integrate these three levels. Although other activities accomplish this task, none of them has integration as its defining purpose. **Transcendence**, or "larger than," is central to this evolving definition of religion, although it takes on more complex connotations in the context of developed religious thinking. Communities are larger than individuals. God is a word always used to point to some inclusive reality much larger than one's self or the varied communities essential to life. At its heart, the function of religion defined this way is to enable human individuals to recognize, accept, know, and relate to those aspects of reality that transcend individuality.

Transcendence has many aspects; a few may be mentioned. We know transcendence from the passage of time and from noticing change and movement. The experiences of difference and contrast, tension and marked stability, may lead to feelings of transcendence. When one experiences "larger than" or " bigger than" or "longer than" or "more inclusive than," one is touching transcendence. At more complex levels, one can experience transcendence by holding two or more interpretations of life and reality in his or her imagination at the same time. All memories of the past and imaginings of the future involve a transcending of the present. Movement and change in human living are what we call growing and aging. As humans age, they participate in the larger or transcendent process of creativity that permeates our universe.

I suggest that the creativity of our Universe is the most inclusive and concrete transcendence that every human being may experience. There are other transcendent entities that some people know—God is one of them—but an increasing number of people alive today have no way to access them. With this brief introduction to the reality of transcendence, let me rephrase the basic meaning and function of religion.

Religion is what individuals and communities of individuals do with the fact of individual human solitariness and their awareness of this condition. The religious response to solitariness deepens and enriches our self knowledge, our need of and involvement in community, and our embeddedness in the creation and creativity of our Universe. Solitariness points to the fact that every individual human lives but once and no one else can do it as a stand-in. Although friends and companions may surround you, only you really suffer the trials and tribulations and delight in the joys and jubilations of your living.

In this definition I substitute the phrase "creativity of the Universe" for the word **God,** which means the constant change that is part of every moment and duration of time. Creativity has two aspects: one moving toward complexity, the other moving toward simplicity. We humans know this creativity as we grow, age, move. Living for all organisms is dependent upon both aspects of creativity. It is a paradox that both aspects of creativity may be good or bad depending on who or what is benefiting from the change.

Whitehead did not equate the terms God and Creativity. **Creativity** is a fundamental category of his thought, defined as "the one becoming the many and the many becoming the one." Creativity is change which may be understood as things coming together into a unity or as one entity breaking apart into elements. It is through consideration of all aspects of creativity that Whitehead leads us to God. Creativity and God are not the same, and some religions make a major distinction between them. The context for this essay is culture that is responding to the increasing power of the secular worldview. Therefore, religion must be defined so that God *may* be at the center of religion, but one may also be religious without reference to God.

I came to understand Whitehead 30 years ago. Since that time I have concluded that it is by considering the creativity of our Universe that we humans may be led to the concept of God. One may know creativity and still not reach God. However, I have come to believe that, as we experience change and reflect upon and wonder about the passage of time, we humans may become concerned about religion and matters religious. Another way to define religion is to say **religion** seeks to give us acceptance and understanding of change through which we may know and cope with the creativity of the Universe.

Time, as known through change, is one reference system of transcendence that every human experiences as growing and aging. This is how the creativity of our Universe is immanent in and through us. As we take seriously birth, change and time, growth and aging, living and dying, life and our own death, the concerns of religion become interesting to us.

Community and the creativity of our Universe are *larger than* the self or any individual. They transcend self. Religion's task is to enable every individual to acknowledge, accept, and understand those aspects of life that transcend the individual. Every viable religion seeks to enable individuals to celebrate, live with and within, the transcendent context of their existence. A well-functioning religion enables individuals to accept and live healthy lives with full appreciation of their personal solitariness within the transcendent aspects of reality, a reality upon which they depend and which they must trust. Religions seek to bring meaning into human living by dealing with how humans interact with what transcends them. Each religion in its own way celebrates the most inclusive realm of transcendence that is relevant to the lives of its followers. Between each person and the most inclusive transcendent reference that the individual knows and accepts as real are many levels of transcendence.

Every religion, recognized as major or minor at the end of the twentieth century, seeks to integrate all the transcendent reference systems of meaning that its tradition identifies and celebrates. Christianity seeks to relate each person to God through the Bible, preaching, worshipping, going to church, and using the story of Jesus as the Christ. Judaism seeks to give meaning to every individual's living by using tradition, study of the Torah, and participation in community. Both of these major traditions understand individuals to live within the context of the creation and creativity of our world. Both help people deal with living and dying, sharing and grieving, success and failure, love and rejection. Both know human beings live in a reality that includes situations in which one is in-control and in which one is helpless. Religion reaches out from the individual to all the circumstances and experiences of life and seeks to bring acceptance, meaning, and affirmation to human living.

In contrast, secular activities and concerns do not have as their primary and essential focus dealing with the transcendent and transcending levels of reality. Secular knowing depends upon the aspect of reason that tends to reduce or deconstruct rather than to integrate and see the whole or the inclusive context. Secular knowing is powerful and generates knowledge because it separates and seeks the smallest part or simplest relationship.

I am sure many readers will quickly deny this distinction with some heat because numerous secular activities and concepts do integrate and take the big picture into account. However, I stand by this distinction. Religion has transcendence as its central and primary concern, relating it to individuals with dramatic and sustaining meaning. Religion seeks to enhance our ability to accept and trust. Secular knowing has identifying facts in the smallest or simplest form as its main concern, in order for us gain knowledge, the capacity to predict, and the power to control.

What distinguishes religion from all other human activities that give meaning to living is the conscious inclusion of self, community, and the transcendent. A family, career, or cause may give purpose and focus to living and create a community, but these are secondary effects of the activity. As essential to their purpose, they do not enable humans to cope with

> aging, illness, dying, and death,
> loss, alienation, and grief,
> birth, love, and marriage,
> anger, rage, guilt, and shame,
> forgiveness and love,
> power and helplessness,
> good and evil,
> loss and change,
> fairness and justice,
> joy and sorrow,
> doubt and faith,
> despair and hope.

We come to know most of these conditions in our personal solitariness. As we reflect upon them, our understanding of transcendence may emerge and transform us into religious persons. In response to feeling solitary, we may seek out a religious community to confirm that we are not alone in the way we accept and move through these ways of being human. It is very lonely without a community that affirms and validates the way one copes with these all too human concerns and experiences. One becomes religious as self, community, and the transcendent dimensions of one's living are included in the resolution reached, nurtured, and celebrated.

Transcendence is central and crucial to religion. I venture to say that **religion** is what individuals and communities do with experiences of transcendence. Without the experience of transcendence, we humans remain unaware of our solitariness. Contrast is needed to give the knowledge of solitariness clarity and depth.

Transcendence means larger than. Human beings have many basic experiences involving transcendence. To cry, to laugh, to feel lucky or unlucky, to feel wonder or awe, to feel guilt or shame, to feel uplifted or fulfilled—all involve transcending the present moment. Much of the time we move through these experiences and that is all there is to it. Nothing comes of them when little or no reflection occurs. Reflection will be needed if the transcendent aspect is to lead to religion.

Individuals learn as they mature that they are dependent on things outside of themselves. Hence, they must also learn to trust. As children we learn how to get along with other humans. As teenagers most of us learn how lonely it is to "go it alone." And, sooner or later, most human beings realize that they need a community to avoid feeling lonely or overwhelmed by the experiences of solitariness. Community is larger than the individual and, therefore, is a transcendent level of the reality in which human beings live.

This is one of the central reasons people go to and join a religious community. In their religious community, they find others who understand the world as they do, who are like they are. There they find acceptance of self by others. When a crisis of living comes, others there have been through it, and coped in a way that made sense, serving unintentionally as models. By being a fellow member, I know that I am not alone. I find support in times of stress.

The experience of transcendence heightens our feelings of solitariness. As we come to know ourselves as solitary within the transcendent creativity of our Universe, we may realize that we need to be in community. Sharing common experiences and interpretations of what our lives mean with other human beings is the glue that bonds a community together. It is the basis of religious community.

My whole career was spent serving religious congregations in the humanist tradition. Within each of them I found the theological perspectives known as humanism, naturalism, mysticism, and theism. Each perspective named a different most *inclusive transcendent reference system of meaning*. God is the reference for theists. Mystics have an experience of "union with the transcendent" that defines their religious perspective. Naturalists relate to the realm of nature. The human community is the reference for humanists. From within our secular culture, the path that leads to human awareness of transcendence is reflection on the ways each human experiences and participates in the creativity of the Universe. For people embedded in secular culture, focusing on how they live within the creativity that transcends them is a way to open them to religious concerns. The religious issues of trust, dependence, power, helplessness, sin, forgiveness, and thankfulness arise from reflection on our human participation in creativity.

Every religion's purpose is to enable individuals to live with their solitariness. This solitariness exists within the context of the transcendent and transcending systems of relationships. What each person experiences, accepts, and knows determines what transcendent relationships his or her religion needs to include. Religions have power to influence human living, as they are relevant to life as individuals experience it. If the understandings, faith, and hope a religion offers do not connect with the experiences of the world—with the way humans need to cope with change and death, the creativity of our Universe—then the religion will be ignored or discarded as incoherent and inapplicable. It will be judged unrealistic, not worth any time or effort.

The intent of the chapters to follow is to enhance every religion's capacity to be vital and vibrant in the lives of human beings today and in the years to come.

Chapter 4

Four Expectations
of Functional Religion

To recap the framework discussed previously, I have defined religion as what individuals do with their solitariness in order to know and integrate how the self needs and participates in community and is embedded in the creativity of our Universe. Implicit to this definition is that religion begins with individuals in relation to ever-larger systems of reference, which are larger than or transcend the self, which I call the **transcendent** or **transcending reference systems**. Of the many ways to conceive of these reference systems of transcendence, the series one chooses depends on the concern that one is pursuing. One such series is self, family, human community, the world of nature, ideas, and creativity (God). Each level transcends (is larger than) the one listed before it. This is functional perspective. In it, religion's task is to discover, know, and celebrate the ways all levels are related in terms of structure and process. Meaning for humans derives from these systems of transcendent reference. Individuals refer to them to know the order, meaning, and purpose of living.

From within this functional understanding of religion, how will we know if a given religion, or activity that claims to be religious, is really fulfilling the religious needs of a community of individuals? Is there a way to compare the effectiveness of differing religions? Is there a standard against which a religion may be judged and found either wanting or vital and dynamic?

I suggest that there are four expectations, which all religions must strive to meet. They are realistic, relative, rational, and reverent. What do I mean by each of these adjectives? Briefly, a **realistic** religion must be adequate and applicable; a relative one must be relevant to the time, space, ethnic traditions, culture, and living of individuals, as well as to communities of them; one that is **rational** must be consistent and coherent; and, if reverent, a religion must constantly work at bringing transcendent perspective and proportion to human living. I have derived the definitions of realistic and rational from those given in the introduction to *Process and Reality*, by Alfred North Whitehead. By examining a religion's content and actual practice we may judge how it brings spiritual health to individuals and communities.

Realistic as a Standard Expectation

Realistic implies that a religion makes sense of human living, based on empirical knowledge. Religion must bring order, understanding, acceptance, and hope to the condition of being human. A religion is adequate if it deals with the complete range of human experience from birth to death, love to grief, freedom to oppression, war to peace. A religion is inadequate if it does not enable human beings to cope with some experience encountered during life. Applicability has to do with how the ideas and practices of a religion address living within the world as both the world and individual change over time. Vitality sustained over several generations is a strong measure of adequacy and applicability.

All of the traditional religions of today are being challenged because so many people are finding religious ideas and practices inadequate or inapplicable to their secular worldview. A definition of religion that depends upon the idea of a supernatural being is inapplicable when secular education and scientific technology dominate our way of knowing and interacting with each other and all elements of our world. The secular worldview has only the natural world for us to know. If humans beings are unable to make the connection between the words which express the ideas and understandings of a religion with real experiences they have had, then the religion does not apply to the world of human living in the present and future. This religion has a problem of integrity, and probably of survival, in the long run.

To insist that religions be realistic is to insist that they be grounded in actual human experience. It accepts that the world in which we humans live is very complex and, therefore, many ways to know and interpret it are valid. To be realistic while living in a big city is very different from being realistic while living in a forest or desert or in mountains. Human male ways of being realistic and interacting with the world are very different from female ways. My wife likes to go shopping by just looking; I find this activity boring. She likes to look at all the things we walk by in a store. I want to get to the thing I came to buy. Looking at things I am uninterested in buying today is of little interest to me.

Many religions and cultures have survival value, demonstrated by the existence of all our world's religious traditions. Each has given meaning to the lives of many human generations by interpreting the transcendent reality in which people live. Every religion has a way of knowing, using reality, and its own metaphysics or paradigm, as does Science. Any religion may have been adequate and applicable at one time, but later not necessarily so. Every religion is dependent on an historical and cultural context; if that context changes, the religion must change or fade away.

Secular values are gaining influence in our lives. During the next decades, some religious traditions may wither and die because they are unable to maintain a realistic perspective and response within the secular world.

Relative as a Standard Expectation

I draw the demand for being relative from Relativity Theory in a metaphorical way. No one religion carries absolute Truth for all times and all peoples. For any given individual, for every community of faith, there is an historical and cultural context that dictates which religious truths will be adequate and applicable to his or her living. For instance I live in America as the twenty-first century begins. That is my historical and cultural context. I may study religions from other times and centuries and cultures, but they will lack relevance for me. They will be lacking in power to speak and bring meaning to my living. I may find some of their insights and rituals to be beneficial, but their full meaning will be lost by having been taken out of their cultural context.

People who are alive as the twenty-first century begins need a religion that adequately makes sense of their experiences of living within the secular world. We need a religion whose insights, faith, and hope may be powerfully applied to the stress, tension, and fast-paced living in our modern world of travel by flight, communication by phone and Internet, news by TV and satellite. We need a religion that is expressed in words and ideas drawn from our worldview. This means that ideas, which have been powerful for generations, may have to be expressed in new ways.

I do not believe that the human condition has changed greatly in the last 50 years, although some members of the Boomer and X generations act as if it has. The stage and context of human living has shifted, but our fundamental needs for meaning, health, faith, hope, love, community, purpose, security, food, clothing, shelter, peace, justice, have not changed. It is just that aspects of the secular world obscure them, as these examples indicate: material things and our feelings of ownership, our feelings of power and control over things and events, our ideals of freedom, and our diminished sense of boundaries and limits. What is so prominent in our secular world obscures basic human needs.

Rational as a Standard Expectation

Reason is a frequently used word today; however, the variety of meanings given this most important of words is confusing. To be **rational** is to be good. If you are in a Christian church, you will be considered rational if you agree with the doctrine of the church. If you work for a corporation, you are considered rational if your decision results in a profit. If you understand science as I do, then you are rational, but if you get emotional, you are irrational. Most of all, you are rational when you agree with me. One may be rational in our society in many other ways. My point is that all these meanings of the word beg for clarity.

I ask that we separate what it means to be reasonable from what it means to be realistic and reverent. Distinguishing these three human mental abilities will give us greater power to understand and analyze our world and ourselves. Each of these three central human capacities has two essential elements. It is as we use each separately and all six as compliments of each other that the full richness of our human interaction with our world will be realized.

I will use reason in a specific way. **Reason** is our human capacity to think and act with consistency and coherence. Consistency means without contradiction, but does not exclude paradox. Coherence means that all the needed pieces are present and fit together. Coherence builds upon adequacy.

In secular practice, the use of reason connotes a tendency toward ordering, categorizing, deconstructing, or taking apart to identify the smallest or simplest element. If there are two explanations of an event, then the simplest one is to be preferred as more elegant or more reasonable. This preference is drawn from one of the postulates of the scientific method. Reason may also have to do with finding and knowing how the outcomes of events repeat themselves. By studying them, we may take them into the realm of public discourse.

Distinctions about Reason

When we use reason in this way, we need make several distinctions. First let me introduce the idea of **non-rational**. Most things, entities, in our world simply are. They may be said to have many characteristics, but consistency and coherence are not among them. A chair is comfortable, functional, and may be appropriate for the room it is in. To use reason to describe it is inappropriate. I submit that emotions are the same. A person has them. If you have ever been in an intimate relationship with someone who is angry, that is a fact you must deal with. To label anger as irrational is neither helpful nor appropriate. In fact, it is unrealistic. More seriously, in reality it is a "put down" of that person's integrity and a blatant reach for power over that person. The level of anger with which a person reacts to a given situation may seem exaggerated and inappropriate to other people; however, the feelings of another person cannot be denied as somehow not a fact.

I am making a significant distinction between reason and reality. Reason does not describe reality. Reason has everything to do with whether the words, ideas, and actions of a human being or group of human beings are *consistent* in these ways:

- with an internally agreed upon set of values;
- within the limits set by the identity of a community or culture;
- with a particular understanding of reality.

To give an extreme case, suppose a person is paranoid and believes he has super powers. His action to crush all threats is then rational. However, if the same person perceives himself as weak and helpless, then hiding under something is a reasonable response to the world which appears threatening. Or again, if the Roman Catholic Church is an integral part of your life, then going to Mass is a rational activity. However, if you are a Protestant or Jew, then going to Mass is inconsistent with the meaning of your living and is, therefore, irrational.

There is a profound difference between using reason and being realistic. In the society in which I live, this distinction is ignored frequently. It is good to be judged reasonable or rational. However, most of the time in conversation, no distinction is made between being reasonable and being realistic.

One of the implications of this understanding and definition is that all sustainable religions are both realistic and rational. Each makes its own selective interpretation of the world in which its followers live, and then proceeds with consistency and coherence to give transcendent meaning to the living of those in community who choose to be its followers. The difference between religions has to do with how they are realistic, *not* with whether each is rational. This difference has to do with whether they are adequate and applicable for human survival, vitality, and vibrance. The tension between any religious faith and science in our secular world has more to do with how each side chooses to be realistic about our world than whether one is rational and the other not.

It is this distinction between being realistic and rational that prompted my insight that true **intellectual freedom** is the capacity to shift metaphysics or perspectives of reality. If one can only reflect and respond to life from within one paradigm or understanding of reality, then you are severely limited in how you may approach the complexity of our world and how you may relate to people holding different perspectives of reality. If you can shift from one interpretation of reality to another with empathy and understanding, then you have a freedom based in intellectual capacity. This implies a freedom of action and relationship beyond the realm of ideas.

The reality in which religion operates must never neglect the transcendent dimension of events or relationships. In fact some religions begin by saying that God is the ultimate transcendent reality and it is here that everything begins. Our human task for these religions is to come to terms with this fact and sustain spiritual health. A more common beginning point for religious reflection in our secular society is the individual. From this starting point, the task is to reach out to that which is transcending of the individual, the moment, the facts.

Between these two very different ways of being realistic, the middle position is to recognize that the first task of religion is to give importance to the relationship of every individual to the *most inclusive transcendent dimension of reality* he or she acknowledges. Secondarily, religion then constructs and sustains a rational set of values within this context. For some individuals today, religion may have to begin by naming levels of transcendence and bringing them into individual experience and consciousness.

My first insight that connected reason and consistency occurred in theological school while reading Whitehead. I was too busy to follow up on it then. However, after graduation this connection kept coming back to inform me and haunt me. I came to see how I was rational in my arguments with my wife, but to also understand how she was just as rational in her arguments with me. As a father I realized that I held values based on years of experience unavailable to my children. From their view of the world, they were as rational as I was.

Further realizations of rationality extended from my family to conflicts tearing apart other regions of the world. Both sides of the Troubles in Ireland, for instance, are rational from within the fear, distrust, and experience of history that potential and actual combatants carry into the present. In the Middle East, both the Israelis and Palestinians are rational from within the value systems that define each as a people who lay claim to the same land. I began to understand that where there are political differences, war and killing maybe a rational end result. This happens when two sides are consistent in their drives for goals. When indigenous in-groups cannot forget or let go of past insults and injuries, compromise is impossible. For terrorism, war, hate, and fear to end, trust must be rekindled. The rational consequences of fear and hate must be interrupted.

If we are an objective third party viewing two other parties who are in conflict, and we clearly separate how each party is being realistic and rational within its own value system, we then have an opportunity to invite both of them to negotiate their differences. The possibility of compromise leading to resolution is opened by changing the reality, or changing the understanding or perception of reality, or by modifying some of the motivating values held by each side.

All of these conclusions have led me to be uncomfortable with the position that to be rational is good. I seldom encounter a person who is not being rational within their understanding of the world. I meet many people who live within a different view of reality from mine. Sometimes the difference is only one value that operates with enough power to make a great deal of difference.

Accepting consistency as central to being rational has another consequence. If a human being takes any value and uses it with absolute consistency, the result will be either unhealthy or absurd. One needs to know when *enough is enough*. For example, eating is good for human beings, however, illness will follow if one eats too much and does not pay attention to body signals that indicate "enough." Every human I know likes to win. If you allow winning to be everything and cheat to gain the highest score so you can be called the winner, you have rendered "winning" meaningless. Placing first in the announced list of results does not demonstrate that you are really the winner because you know you cheated, and that renders the experience absurd.

If anger at another is governed by the consistency of reason, that anger easily leads to rage with killing its focus as the only end. Political competition will always lead to war, unless there is a sense of limits and when *enough is enough*. Arguments between two people who really care for each other will go on forever if one does not have a sense of, "It is enough!" Without a sense of enough within our human community, we would not have forgiveness, thankfulness, mercy, compassion, or justice. Only if one has a sense of when enough is enough will the absurd, which may consume our living, be kept in check. Without a sense of enough, the ideal of perfection and the desire for control will lure us into patterns of living that are unhealthy and destructive. The bonds of family and community depend upon acceptance of limits to individualism. They depend on everyone agreeing on when *enough is enough*. Human spiritual health depends on it, too.

This sense of enough resolved for me the riddle of God as the First Cause. There is an ancient proof for the existence of God. It begins by observing that everything in our world has a cause, therefore everything else must have a cause as well. **God** is defined as the first cause of everything else. Our modern rational mind asks what is the cause of the first cause? And what is the cause of the cause of the first cause? The consistency of reason dictates that one should not stop with God. However, several hundred years ago when this proof of God's existence was suggested, it was enough to explain the world and stop the absurd progression.

So I now suggest that our human use of reason needs to be used with an ever-present sense of enough. I sometimes speak of the **Enough Principle**. Invoking it for myself and for the groups with whom I am engaged contributes very positively to my health and to peace in my interpersonal relationships. For years I have wondered what is the source of the Enough Principle? Does it stand alone? Is it related to something else? Does its power and relevance derive from some source? How does one know when to apply it? The answer to this question is that the Enough Principle comes from our sense of reverence.

Reverence as a Standard Expectation

One afternoon while thinking about reverence as perspective and a sense of proportion, I realized that the sense of enough is rooted in our capacity for reverence. For some people, reverence is rooted in awe and wonder. I agree that these emotions are one aspect of reverence, but I believe they result from it rather than define it. I have come to understand this most important word differently. Reverence is important because its use is what keeps reason from taking us to the absurd. Reverence is also the path that leads to knowing transcendence.

I have carried the title of Reverend for some 30 years now. One quiet winter day I got to wondering what it is that I, as a Reverend, bring to any community. What is it that any Reverend is supposed to bring to the community he or she serves? Some Reverends bring the dogma or creeds of their religion. That is the content of what they bring. Remember that I am asking this question from outside a Christian or Jewish community. I am asking what does any Reverend or Rabbi, regardless of dominant community characteristic, bring that justifies giving appropriate deference to that person.

From within the framework of functional religious understanding, there are two essential elements of **reverence,** namely, perspective and proportion. Every religious leader is given deference because he or she is expected to bring and maintain a sense of transcendent perspective and proportion within the community being served.

A clergy person will be sought out for advice on a matter of ethics because seekers expect clergy to respond with values that transcend self-interest. The advice given by a member of the clergy is expected to be grounded in community, or come from God, or be informed by religious wisdom and tradition. All these should bring a sense of transcendent perspective and proportion to self-interest.

The meaning of **perspective**, as I use it, is an understanding of living that always includes some of the many layers of transcendence within and upon which living individuals depend. Any selected religion will include many layers of transcendence and exclude others. Every religion will give a particular interpretation to the layers of transcendence it uses to give order, meaning, and purpose to the life experiences of human beings.

Proportion to me means a wisdom that maintains healthful tension and an appropriate sense of balance. At one end of the continuum is each human self living within assembled communities; at the other, are transcending reference systems of meaning that sustain and nourish vitality and vibrance, faith, hope, and capacity for love. In the middle (on the fulcrum) is our sense of proportion that relates these ends to each other.

I am suggesting that perspective and proportion are the basis from which reverence begins. Without them, reverence is absent. Many people associate reverence with awe and wonder in moments of intense reverence. These feelings are one form reverence may take. Why does anyone feel awe and wonder? I suggest that awe and wonder follow from one's sense of transcendent perspective and proportion. There are many other ways humans are reverent.

The use of reverence in realms of human concern is needed to keep our all-too- human use of reason from going too far. The use of reverence brings in and applies the Enough Principle. Only as we humans have and use a sense of perspective and proportion will we keep our survival instinct and our drives for security, power, wealth and control within limits that are peaceful and healthy. Without reverence (perspective and proportion), our lives will be dominated by frustration becoming anger, and anger becoming rage, and rage leading to war, and war without mercy or compassion. Without reverence, perspective, and proportion, our need for security will lead us to accumulate wealth, and this in turn will lead to greed that corrupts any happiness security brings. Without reverence our sense of justice will be corrupted into vengeance. Without reverence there will be no forgiveness, thankfulness, acceptance, fulfillment, peace of mind, satisfaction, happiness, joy, appreciation in our living. I believe that each of these depends upon a sense of perspective and proportion which balances the needs of individuals within the transcending reference systems of meaning within which they live.

Each of the relationships listed below includes transcendence as a crucial element. These are some of the relationships reverence brings to our awareness. The task of religion is to give to every individual's life order and meaning, understanding and acceptance, faith, and hope. In fulfilling this task every religion must strive to be realistic and relevant, rational and reverent. Every religion should strive to relate these entities in whatever form they exist:

> Every individual to community,
> In-groups to humanity,
> Humanity to the creativity,
> The human community to God,
> Our feelings of Power to helplessness,
> Control to boundaries,
> Enough to perfection,
> Faith to works,
> Love and grief,
> Laughter and tears,
> Living and dying,
> Growing and aging,
> Stability and change,
> I to you,
>> We to them,
>> I to Thou,
> Good to evil,
> Benedictions to maledictions,
> Freedom to determinism,
>> The present to the past and future,
>> The concrete to the abstract,
>> The specific to the general,
> An event to that which transcends it.

Perspective sets the context and a sense of proportion tells us what to do with the implications of the context. A sense of proportion is the way we humans may resolve tension, conflict, paradox, stress, contrast, and priorities of values.

I believe that secular society praises the use of reason to the neglect of reverence. Human spiritual and physical health will improve as the use of reverence is given equal honor in our living.

Chapter 5

Functional Concerns for Religious Diversity: An Overview

In the last few pages I tried to set forth an understanding of religion expressed in functional terms instead of with definitions dependent upon the content of a limited range of Christianity. I have suggested that if the English language is to be used with integrity within our modern world then the definitions found in dictionaries need to be broader so that they apply to all religions and religious activities. Implicit in these pages has been the belief that religion is relevant to our human condition no matter what ethnic tradition and community is considered. I have said that religion is distinguished from other human activities in the way it seeks to name, organize, and integrate the transcendent reference systems of entities, which surround every individual. Religion lifts human relatedness within time and entities (things) to the level of meaning.

Religion has two sides: activity and worship, symbols and theology. The action side includes singing, preaching, reading, liturgy, worship, prayer, meditation, etc. Theology is the reflective side expressed in words.

Functional Theology

The dictionary defines theology as the study of "man's relationship to God." I suggest a broader definition. **Theology** defined functionally is the study of the ways human beings use transcending systems of entities to establish and sustain meaning that gives health, vitality and vibrance, faith and hope to their living. Theology means human reflection using memory and imagination about how individuals and communities relate to the transcending and transcendent reference systems of meaning within which living takes place. This is another way of saying that theology is how human beings put into words and symbols what they have done with their solitariness.

I believe Christian theology is an example of this. I believe this is what the study of the Torah is all about. This definition is broad enough, but narrow enough, to enable us to know what is theological and what is not. At this point one should remember that any theological reflection should be realistic to a specific community and its traditions. And, if it is to have applicability, it will sustain life from one generation to the next, using both reason and reverence so that the meaning and health of the living individuals served has vitality and vibrance.

Functional Religion

Religion is what individuals do with their solitariness. It is how human beings integrate and live with the ever-growing experiences of self, their individual dependence within community, and each person's participation in the creativity of our Universe. When religion is understood this way, there are several concerns to which I think all religions must respond. Each of these concerns follows from universal human experiences typical of our human condition. I believe that all the established world religions, in fact, respond to these concerns. If a new religion is to be successful and meet the complex needs for meaning over many generations of people, it must respond to these concerns.

These religious concerns may be separated into seven or more areas of generally related issues. Each area will begin with our basic definition of religion and then set forth a cluster of issues that flow from some aspect of our condition of being human. I believe each of these areas and the proposed range of responses are based in experiences, which are real within secular culture. Many of them will be found to be common to all cultures and human beings. Every religion will have its interpretation, which is dependent upon the cultural context and tradition, to bring meaning to individuals living in communities.

Even though reflection in one area will overlap into others, I think that each has a focus that justifies the separation. Every area is also interdependent with the others in some ways. However, clarity of understanding and increased power of application warrants some sorting of the issues.

I suspect that there will be two groups of people who will feel some discomfort with stretching traditional definitions of theological terms. First will be Christians who will feel no need to do this. They are comfortable with the traditional definitions found in dictionaries. The second group includes those who have grown up in secular culture and who carry intellectual and emotional scars associated with Christian theological words and ideas. To both I say, the task before us is to create a theological understanding that is relevant and vital within secular culture and to our human condition. There are two choices as I see it:

1.   *Invent a new set of words*, and ask everybody to learn
      a new jargon.

2.   *Work from tradition*, recognize its validity and power, and
      expand the meaning of some words; ground the new
      understandings in readily identifiable experiences.

Learning a new jargon probably is not high on anyone's list of priorities. My professional career as a minister taught me that ordinary people, who neither teach nor write for a living, have a low tolerance for that kind of activity. You may also have noticed that long, unintelligible words are not my strong suit. Based on my experience of learning new words to express old ideas in philosophy, however, I choose the second option. Words after all, said a competitor in *Alice in Wonderland*, mean what we say they mean. I do not intend to destroy the house of traditional religion, but to redecorate or renovate it. People who live within secular culture should know that the religious dimension of our human living is their home too. They ignore or discount it at their peril.

Seven Areas of Religious Concern

Below, I name seven areas drawn from traditional theology and redefine each in terms of a general function within our human condition. Each new definition is based on human experience. Doing this, I believe, renders the response of any religion as an example of how a particular function maybe fulfilled.

1. Soteriology: the study of salvation; how humans respond to death
2. Ontology: the study of being, doing, and power
3. Eschatology: the study of last things, time, and change
4. Metaphysics: the study of what is real
5. Ethics: the study of values, morality, good and evil, right and wrong
6. Christology: the study of how religions use symbols
7. Epistemology: the study of how we gain religious knowledge

During and after introducing these seven areas of theological concern in succeeding chapters, I will suggest that there are four faiths defined by the language individuals use to discuss these concerns. All four are fully functional within secular culture. Each has strengths and weaknesses. Each emerges out of the way individuals experience and respond to living in our world. The four faiths are humanist, naturalist, mystic, and theist, each with several options or derivations. Nevertheless, individuals in each group use language in very similar ways and have common experiences and responses to living.

Other areas of theological concern also may exist. One friend has suggested Ecclesiology to deal with how religious communities are organized and governed. For the purposes of this book, seven is enough. I leave additions for others or, perhaps, another time.

Chapter 6

Soteriology

Soteriology is the branch of theology that is concerned with salvation. My *American Heritage Dictionary* (p.1594) gives this definition for salvation:

1.a.   preservation or deliverance from destruction, difficulty, or evil...
2.   Theology. a. Deliverance from the power of sin: redemption....

Salvation is the central concern of many Christians. Therefore, by this definition, sin is the central concern of Christianity. The dictionary definition is given in the content of Christianity; however, if one's religious understanding of human living does not find sin to be the central issue of life, this definition is rather useless.

All during the years I was growing up in Oklahoma and then during the eight years I was a minister in Arkansas, one of the first questions I was asked upon meeting someone was, "Are you saved?" As a Unitarian Universalist I knew I was not saved in the way my new acquaintance wanted me to be. I did not accept Jesus as the Christ in the way their branch of Christianity did. I used to take a deep breath, and answered with integrity, "No!" It was always interesting to find out how this would affect the next few minutes of conversation or the possibility of friendship.

One afternoon I was asked this question again and got to thinking about it. I asked myself why this question is so important? Why am I so different if my answer is no? What does accepting Jesus as the Christ do for all the people who are obviously concerned about my present state? After some reflection I concluded that accepting Jesus as the Christ provides people with hope for life after death. If this acceptance is fully functional, they no longer fear dying because living which ends in death is understood to have meaning. Death is a transition to "life after death." This gives life and death meaning to Christians who fully believe this teaching.

The question, "Are you saved?" was really three questions rolled into one. First, are you a Christian? Second, are you one of us? and third, have you resolved how to live with the full knowledge and acceptance of death as the end of life?

The acceptance of Jesus as the Christ is one resolution of how to live with the knowledge of death faced by every human being. Children tend to be innocent of this concern. Youth tend to live as if they are immortal. Young men, and now women, drive cars too fast. Young adults tend to take risks that older people do not. When I was in my early twenties, I climbed rocks and mountains with little or no sense of the risk to life and limb. Only as Americans reach about the age of 30, do they deal fully with their feelings that they are mortal, maybe "over the hill," and that death will actually happen to them.

Over the years I have come to use the term "**saved**" for anyone who has resolved to live with vitality and vibrance, faith and hope, after fully accepting that death is part of life, is the end of living, and is going to happen to them. **Soteriology** is the study of how individuals and communities resolve to go on living in spite of death, illness, and despair. One of the central functions of religion is to establish and sustain for individuals within a community that living is worthwhile in spite of death. A person is saved when he or she has resolved the issues that follow from knowing that death is part of living. After realizing this and accepting it, I have answered the question, "Are you saved?" with a "Yes!" even though I know that my way of salvation does not fall under many of the interpretations Christians use. If I want to spark discussion, I may add an opening, "Yes, I am saved, but not the way you mean."

The way individuals sustain salvation is to connect with that which transcends them. We become involved with a community such as a church, city, school, or corporation. We participate in a cause or political party. We give our lives serving others, family members, friends, those in need.

Salvation answers the functional question of how human beings affirm living in spite of the reality that life depends on and ends in death. Here are some of ways to ask the question of salvation:

- How will you live your life?
- For what are you giving your life?
- For what values are you giving your life each day?
- What level of peace with your soul do you have at the end of each day?
- What values and style will you give to your living, beginning with tomorrow's dawn?

One of the dramatic ways I have opened this concern for people is to ask, "What do you believe happens at death?" Many people who are deeply involved in secular culture have not thought about this question. They have never talked about it or sat down with others who have the same doubts and level of discomfort with this concern. A great deal of denying death is typical of secular American-European culture because that culture fails to accept death realistically as fundamental to living.

To the blunt question, "what do you believe happens when we humans die?" many people will say they don't know or that it is an unanswerable question. While it is true that no one has a memory of this event, some people have had near-death experiences. However, after some reflection on my years studying philosophy and theology and practicing ministry, I suggest that there are only three broad answers available to us from within the human imagination. All the answers to death, given by the religions I know of, fall into one of these possibilities:

1. Life after death
2. When you die, you are dead; death is the end of you
3. Reincarnation.

Over nine years and in six congregations, I have made this suggestion and invited anyone to add other options to these three possibilities. Surely the creativity of workshop participants is not limited! If they could have conceived of others, this list would be longer, but no one has done so. I now feel fairly confident that these possibilities are the only ones open to us from within the human imagination about what happens at death.

Christianity is clearly an example of faith in an afterlife. Hinduism is an example of faith in reincarnation. If you understand human living as operating within an evolutionary context, you may believe that death is the end of an individual's life and accept that the meaning of human life comes through passing on genes and memories to family and friends. One implication of evolution is that we human beings are one element in the food chain, which sustains all forms of life. Living depends on death; however, the Theory of Evolution does not speak to an individual's concern with death and the meaning of living, as religion does. All three of these examples of religious meaning conclude, in a different way, that what a person does with his or her living is important.

Religion's task is to enable men and women to live with zest in spite of the reality that to do so leads to death. Ironically, the more zest one puts into living, the sooner death may come. Are the metaphorical cosmic cards really stacked against us? Within theology, soteriology deals with these concerns.

To enable men and women to love in spite of the knowledge that to do so will bring grief is another aspect of the soteriological function of religion. To sustain the power and meaning of rituals of grieving is yet another soteriological activity of religion. When death causes us grief, we may respond with a "Yes, but..." or "In spite of." The "yes, but" is not full acceptance of death. Usually there is anger and some denial wrapped in this response. "In spite of" implies a very different level of acceptance. I suggest this phrase contains the most important words in theological practice.

Sin and Sins

Many say that the purpose of salvation in Christianity is to save us from our sins. Some branches of Christianity treat sin as a long list of specific acts. I understand sin to be a metaphor drawn from archery. When archery was a very important activity in ancient cultures, a sin was to miss the targeted spot. A **sin** was to aim with full attention and skill at the mark, and then to miss it. If you have ever used a bow and arrow, shot a gun, or thrown a ball, you have experienced how often one intends to hit the chosen mark, but misses it anyway.

Sin is a metaphor that has implications for all human living. All human activity intends or aims at some specific good. Every specific good is thought to contribute to a larger GOOD in life. However, with all our intentions toward achieving the Good, we humans miss it much of the time. We miss the good we intend, thereby missing the good in life. We continually miss the mark we aim at. Or is it that we have aimed at the wrong mark?

What "wrong" marks? We value our individuality too much or are greedy or self-centered. We insist on our rights and neglect our responsibilities. We are driven toward perfection, but hurt others and ourselves in seeking this goal. We have missed the real good of being alive. We learn some activity is fun and brings pleasure or status. We want more and more of it until it becomes an addiction and the ruling passion of our lives. We misuse alcohol or some other drug or some objective thing. We come to know the truth and become too righteous about it. We seek the good in living and miss obtaining it or obtain too much of it. We seek to possess it and control it.

The good in living cannot be possessed or controlled. We always intend the good and pursue it with our reason and miss it. I believe in sin. We are guilty of sin and need to respond to this condition.

Within a Christian context, we humans sin because we fail to follow the laws of God, fail to follow the teachings of Christianity, fail to accept

Jesus as the Christ. The result of sin is two-fold, alienation from God and eternal life in hell after death.

The Christian answer is that one should adopt the Christian faith to lift the consequences of sin and gain the option of life after death by going to heaven. The Christian answer is only one response to this issue. I think there are other answers to how we go on living with the knowledge of death and respond to sin. Death and sin need not be connected, as they are in Christian thought.

As I understand Buddhism, suffering and pain are central concerns of living. To be saved from the suffering that follows from our desires, we humans need to let go of desire. If we can fully let go of all things, even life, we may achieve nirvana and free ourselves from the reincarnational cycle of life and death. This religious answer to living with the knowledge of death is very different than the Christian response.

Many people in secular society believe that death is the end of every individual. There is nothing of consequence after death. What counts is how we live now and how we will be remembered. What contributions did we make? These people believe that every sin in this life has its own consequences in the living of the person sinning. The consequences come in both the material world and in the spiritual realm. We can figure out no cosmic justice from this perspective. Good things happen to bad people and bad things happen to good people. We live by seeking the good and aiming to realize it, knowing we are not in control. Life has meaning because we may know satisfaction, fulfillment, and peace of spirit as we realize the true, the good, the beautiful for ourselves and within the transcendent communities upon which we depend and trust.

Death is accepted as the end of life and as an essential part of living. As Ashley Montagu once said, "We live by dying and when we cease to die, we cease to live." He was speaking about the biochemical processes of building up and tearing down molecules of the substances every life form requires to stay alive. The ultimate in tearing down is death.

Knowing the Good in life follows from knowing when enough is good enough. This humanist or naturalist faith wrestles with the issues of defining the Good and accepting some authority upon which the vision of the Good rests. A host of issues also surrounds concerns of thankfulness and forgiveness. Why should one be thankful? What or who has the power or authority to grant forgiveness to a human being who has sinned?

Soteriology is concerned with how humans respond to death through religion so that living has vitality and vibrance. Each religious faith focuses on an aspect of life as central and proceeds to give human living meaning. I believe soteriological concerns are central to every religion and, when understood functionally, they are universal throughout the human condition. A dialogue between religions is possible by using a set of functional definitions.

Chapter 7

Ontology

The formal definition of ontology in my dictionary is the study of being. As a branch of metaphysics, it is frequently understood to be part of philosophy. My experience with philosophy over the last 40 plus years begins with considerations of our physical world and how we humans understand it. Philosophy has a very objective feel to it. Functional theology, in contrast, has a very personal feel and focus; central to it is what individuals do and have done with their solitariness. Theology *per se* is the study of the patterns of connections that sustain the meaning of life for individuals and communities. In this essay, **theology** is the study of how human beings relate to and within that which transcends them. It is the study of the ways human beings use transcending systems of entities to establish and sustain meaning that gives health, vitality, and vibrance to their living.

Functional **ontology** is concerned with how individuals resolve the tension between doing and being, control and helplessness; with how human beings use their freedom; and, with how they know and sustain a sense of self-worth. Ontology is the study of what it means **to be** human. It has four major concerns at its core:

1. *Being* as opposed to doing
2. *Power and control* versus helplessness
3. *Human freedom*
4. *Dependence and trust*

To consider ontology, let us begin with our functional definition of religion, namely, those human activities concerned with what individuals and their communities do with individual experiences of solitariness. When humans become religious, they reach out from their awareness of solitariness into transcendent reference systems of entities to establish meaning which enables and nourishes health. The focus of this essay is on the issues of what it means to be alive as a human being within secular society.

Being versus Doing

Within our secular society, *being* is opposed to *doing*. You gain worth by what you do. Status is measured by how much power you have as net worth, how much money you earn annually, or how much influence you are thought to wield. How much responsibility you carry for yourself, other people, or an organization or cause has something to do with your worth, but the emphasis tends to be on the material side. Upon meeting someone, people are strongly tempted to ask, "What do you do?" within the first few minutes.

When they were young my children had a hard time understanding that I was working when I sat down to write a sermon. I did not go to work as other daddies did and I was not moving material things around, such as a lawn mower. How could daddy be working sitting in a chair wiggling a pencil or just thinking?

One of the great positive values of secular society is that learning to do something new can "improve" a person's status and value within society. This will increase the respect received from others and impact his or her perception of self-worth. In feudal society, humans knew who they were by what family they were born into and by their birth order and sex. Members of royal families in some European nations still have status by virtue of membership in that family. In America one may have status if one is born into a family of established wealth. One may gain status by gaining wealth, but first-generation wealth is some how different from wealth that has been handed down for several generations. In some Asian societies today a caste system determines who you are in that society.

There is so much to do in our secular society that many people have never confronted the experience of having nothing to do. It seems to me that children today may grow up never having experienced those very long summer afternoons when there seems to be nothing to do. Some people find having nothing to do so devastating that they die within a month or two of retirement because the meaning of their lives is over.

Most people have a job within our system of economic exchange, and this structure defines what is worth doing and fills time with activity. If one becomes self employed, there is a major adjustment. The individual must learn to use freedom to fill time-passing without an external source to define value. These people must create a priority list of things to do, and depend upon their own sense of self-worth to choose what to do, and when enough is enough for today. If you work within a larger organization, it decides what will be done and validates the worth of what you have done through its payroll and benefits systems. If you are self employed, then validation of self-worth must come from an intangible source within yourself. This greater degree of freedom demands doing much more with one's solitariness.

I once went through a period of unemployment. I struggled with how to maintain my sense of self-worth. There was no organization that defined the value of how I spent my days by paying me. I was alive and not doing what I wanted or expected to do. I had to learn how *to be* with self-worth and not depend upon *doing* for my self-worth. Now I am retired and my sense of self-worth comes from what I have done over the past 31 years. I seem to know that it is enough. Something has happened inside of me. I feel a need to be doing things, but not within the structure of a transcendent organization. In both cases, I have more freedom than when I had responsibilities to other people.

If you have been "down sized" from a changing company, you know the terror of waking up to discover that the transcendent reference of meaning derived from what you do is gone. You have thought of yourself as a worker for XYZ corporation or agency or organization for 10 or 15 years or more, contributing to the bottom line and achieving mind-numbing goals. One day you are told, "Leave and don't come back," in polite, euphemistic terms. This experience forces you to face these powerful questions, "Who am I now? What will I do? How will I sustain my sense of self-worth while just being alive each day?"

If someone you love deeply and with whom you are intimately involved has gotten a serious illness or died, you have been confronted with other questions, "What is living worth and why? Have I been doing so much that I have neglected being with those I care for and love, and who love me?"

If you have ever had to decide how much work is enough for today and this week, you have probably struggled with when to accept *enough as enough*. You have known the pressure to work until your living is nothing but work. There is always more to do than can be done. As a minister in this situation, I longed for some time to just be with a clear conscience

At around the age of 30, most individuals in our American-European culture learn of their personal mortality in a way that changes the way they approach living. When we are young teen-agers or in our early twenties, we act as if we are immortal. We know of death, but act as if it will not happen to us. We suffer the Thirty-Year-Old Disease when people the age of 40 and beyond are no longer seen as ancient because we will be there all too soon. This is a theological disease because it has to do with the meaning of life and living. Since I no longer understand my self as a young person who is on the way up, what is the meaning of my living? This is a question of how will I be alive in the future.

This question occurs to most people many times as they go through the stages of adult living. It becomes relevant about every seven to ten years as we age. As the balance of doing and being in our lives shifts in favor of being, the questions of my life's meaning and who am I now emerge to be reworked. I have just retired and no longer will be serving a congregation as minister. I will no longer be *doing* ministry. In terms of ministry the meaning of my living shifts to *being* alive, accepting life as a gift, needing no justification in work.

Being and Self-worth

Anyone who has known oppression or a disability or who has lived with being a negatively-judged minority within a larger group has struggled with the issue of validating his or her own worth. Any experience that raises a significant issue of self identity raises the question, how am I going to be human? Anyone who has felt less capable with age has had to wrestle with how to move beyond deriving the meaning of life by doing. They have had to learn how to accept that living has meaning because one is alive, and caring, and up and about each morning.

This list of examples, which could be much longer, covers a very wide range of traumatic experiences we humans have all had too often. Let me summarize by saying that, sooner or later, these questions arise for every solitary individual:

- Why me?
- Why does my life have worth?
- Why should I carry on with living?
- What is the source of my life's value?
- How do I know that I have enough value to sustain the daily routine of living?

In some cases the question is, why should I not commit suicide? Albert Camus, in his book *The Myth of Sisyphus,* wrote that this is the only question for human beings. Can there ever be only one question or only one religion? In actuality, it is just one more question dealing with what it means "*to be.*"

At one level all humans, all living organisms, have a will to survive. However, if you have experienced depression or grief or despair or a significant loss or major change in your life over which you have little or no control, you know that the will to live may be overcome by the lack of self-worth. Why and how will I be alive as a human being? This is the element of our human condition to which ontology seeks to respond. Martin Luther posed the question as the tension between faith and works. He drove himself sick by trying to validate his self-worth with work. He finally concluded that we humans are saved, find peace of spirit, by faith alone. He meant, of course, the Christian faith. He recognized and came to accept that he could never work enough to feel his life was justified. He came to know that faith is a gift. Faith for Luther meant Christian faith and the knowledge that he was acceptable in the eyes of God.

For modern individuals the question may be, how do I know I am acceptable and accepted within the transcendent world in which I live? If you have never been depressed, the power of this question may have fortunately by-passed you. One can never work hard enough to earn acceptance. One can never work long or hard enough to come to feel he or she deserves peace of spirit. The feeling of self-worth within the transcendent world only comes with faith, as a gift from some transcendent source. The dynamics of this issue of living are the same whether you are Christian, mystic, or humanist.

This gift of knowing you are worthy to be alive comes as a gift. Frequently it comes when one is in the greatest need of it and yet least expects it. It is this experience that some name Grace. I suggest that it is a profound example of grace but not the only one in human living.

The problem within secular culture is that there is little or no acknowledgment of the importance of transcendent reference systems of meaning. One is usually asked, "What can you do for me?" One is taught to do; little is said about *being*. It is this tension that is at issue today as individuals seek spiritual peace and meaning within secular culture.

Asian religions that use breathing meditation to quiet the mind know this truth also. The quieting of the mind and body to the point of stillness leads us to know a state of being with as little doing as is humanly possible. If and when one's mind becomes quiet without distractions, one may learn to be centered and grounded in the transcending reference systems of meaning. A person's sense of time and self shifts. Just being lifts up and gives an experience of self-worth that never comes from doing and worldly success. One learns that having power and possessions are not what give living value and ultimate sustaining worth. A sustaining sense of worth comes as one accepts and celebrates his or her connection to the transcendent. This connection enables one to be.

Control versus Helplessness

A second significant way ontological concerns enter our lives may pose one of the most profound issues of health for our secular society. Essentially it is how every individual resolves to live with the tension between needs for power and control, and his or her experiences of helplessness. Who is in control of my living? How will I respond to all those situations in which I am not in control or to those in which I must trust or am dependent?

This is one of the dividing lines between secular culture and a religious understanding of our human condition. Secular culture has created homes, and cities, and means of travel, and means of communication, in which we feel we are in control. If we are cold, we turn up the heat. If we are too warm, we turn on the air conditioning. If it is dark, we turn on the lights. If we don't like the weather, we travel to some other place where it is more to our liking. If we are hungry, we go to the supermarket and find a seemingly endless variety of food from which to choose. If I need to know something, I go out on the Internet and have access to most of human knowledge and history.

Secular education holds us responsible for what we learn. And what we learn is how to control independent variables so we can predict and control how the dependent variables will react. Much of the advertising in all media seeks to sell us a product because it will give us control over something or some situation. Our homes give us control over a small piece of real estate. The higher our job is in an organization, the more power we are seen as having. How much you have done, are doing, are capable of doing, and are expected to do in the future, measures success in secular culture.

The understanding of reality that religions seek to respond to concerns those situations in life when we are not in control—when we must accept, trust, and are dependent on other human beings and circumstances; when we are completely overwhelmed by natural events such as tornadoes, hurricanes, earthquakes, floods, loss of that which we hold dear, aging, illness, death. Religions ask how will you accept and live in spite of these experiences? How will any human being place these experiences in some pattern that will make what is devastating bearable? What is it that will restore health and vitality to living after the accepted order or pattern of living has been lost or destroyed?

Before I retired at age 62 I was frequently asked, "What will you do then?" This is a secular question. The underlying religious question is, how will you sustain the meaning and value in your sense of living when you are no longer serving as a minister? From the context of the way the question was asked, I sometimes wondered if I was not being asked how could I give up all the power I exercised as an interim minister? All these questions are concerned with the ontological aspect of my human living. They are concerned with how I will be when I give up doing what I have been doing.

For some years I have been leading a workshop which has one session concerning the ontological concerns of religion and our human living. In this workshop I include the following exercise in which I place three headings on a sheet of newsprint: Control, Mixed, and Helpless. Then I invite the participants to suggest personal experiences that fit under each column. Usually someone will respond, "I am in control when I am driving my car, reading a book, and cooking in my kitchen." And someone else will remember how helpless they felt when their mother died and when the river flooded their home three years ago. And someone will say, "I work for our city and I depend on lots of people, yet I have some responsibility to act. I think work goes in the middle column."

Sooner or later someone will observe that driving a car depends on trusting all the other drivers to drive safely and patiently, and say, "I think my sense of control while driving depends on many things." And then someone will observe that reading and cooking depend on other human beings and on the organization and process of our culture working well to provide books, light, energy, and food to us. After some reflection and discussion a all experiences end up in the middle column.

No one has thought of an experience in which there are not elements of trust and dependence; therefore, an individual is not "in control." There seems to be no experience in which we are completely in control or in which we are totally helpless. In every situation where the feeling of helplessness dominates, every person has some power of choice in how to respond.

Within secular culture one way to ask the ontological question is, who or what is in charge of your living? Who or what controls the conditions and choices that make up your living? This question asks us to find an answer in some transcendent reference system. Some people answer, "I am!" and to some extent they are correct. Others say, "We (meaning humanity) are!" Longer responses might start with, "I understand that as a human being I live within the natural world and am dependent upon it. I have some freedom but may use it only within the laws of nature and the conditions set by my—our—history." This is the answer of some naturalists. Theists and mystics know that there is a transcendent context to our living and express a sense of human dependence upon this. Some say, "God is in charge." And some acknowledge the transcendent mystery that they know surrounds all life.

The way any person sorts out the tension between control over life and helplessness over the events of living is an answer to the ontological question of theology. Secular culture seeks to increase how we humans are in control, to give meaning and power to our living by putting us in control, or to keep us busy doing something. Religions accept that trust, dependence, and lack of power and control are ever-present elements of our human condition. They seek to enable individuals and communities to know, accept, and celebrate meaning and goodness in life, in spite of this. Religion fully accepts that all living depends on death and ends in death. It holds on to the faith that living is worthwhile in spite of death.

Human Freedom

Human beings have a sense of freedom, the capacity of choice. At the simplest level our use of freedom concerns whether I turn on a light, or choose to sit or stand. Exercising freedom becomes more important as we choose what we will do with our educational opportunities, who we may marry, whether to have children, and as we choose to respond to living with either "yes, but!" or "in spite of." Choosing "in spite of" implies a more profound level of acceptance than "yes, but!" Freedom underlies our sense of humor, our capacity and willingness to laugh and cry, and our expression of feelings. We exercise freedom as we choose which good we will act toward.

Human freedom is conditioned by each individual's genetic endowment and limited by the conditions surrounding our lives. What we have done in our past testifies to the freedom we believed we had. Memory and imagination also shape and guide how each of us uses our freedom. Education, ethnicity, and religious background may also strongly influence our use of freedom of choice. Every person has a different capacity for free choices.

The capacity for freedom is the source of our human ability to know and respond to that which transcends every individual and the present. Human freedom depends on how we use memory and imagination. It is the capacity to imagine different options for the future and to choose between them. It is our ability to remember and yet not be bound completely by our past. It is freedom that enables us to respond to our solitariness. The capacity for freedom is essential to being human.

Freedom is that capacity to have choices in the present. Freedom still operates even if one can trace the line of causes that led to a choice. Every choice made can be so traced in hindsight to a chain of causes. Freedom is the power to choose which chain of causes in the present will determine the choice this time. Many humans live within established patterns, making their actions very predictable. However, as humans we may learn to change how we respond to situations in life. We have the ability to transcend our past. We have the ability to think and move beyond what we have known and experienced. We humans may look at our world and know good and evil and judge between them. This is using freedom and is one way we transcend our present and ourselves.

Dependence and Trust

Secular culture has a tendency to emphasize individuality and how individuals are free and in control. At he same time it discounts a measure of reality as to how we humans are helpless in the sense of being dependent on circumstances and other people. Every moment of our living is dependent on the world around us. Every moment we must trust. It is when our trust is violated that we acknowledge dependence. It is when our expectations are not met that we suspect we are not in control. Issues of dependence and trust are always with us, yet we seldom probe, reflect on them, and celebrate them adequately. To be concerned with power and control is usually to ignore dependence and trust issues. Religion calls our attention to these elements of the reality of being human.

My intent here is not to resolve all ontological issues. It is to raise the central questions that define a functional theological understanding of ontology. There are many ways this ontological dimension of human living troubles us or raises concerns which ask for a response. Religion responds by understanding that every human being lives within reference systems of meaning that transcend the individual. It is as we humans develop ways of knowing and interacting with these transcendent reference systems that we are religious. They are essential to understanding religion functionally. Ontological concerns cannot be resolved or responded to without them.

Issues of power and control, dependence and trust, are defined and take shape as one considers the transcendent contexts within which an individual lives or uses to define self-worth and the meaning of life. In the examples below, notice how the balance between power and trust, control and dependence, shifts as one reflects on the meaning of self within the *different transcendent reference systems*. There are many ways to describe what I call the transcending reference systems of meaning. Every religion, culture, and style of life creates or uses a matrix of relatedness between individuals and the transcending reference systems of meaning to sustain life and living. Let me suggest several:

1. Self with the self
   Individual within community
   Humanity within the natural world
   Individuals with the realm of ideas
   Individuals and communities within the creativity of our world

2. Self—Community—Tradition—My people—God

3. Self—Family—Job or career—Nation

4. Self—Family—Serving a cause (*e.g.*, freedom, liberation, communism, democracy)

5. Self—Family—Religious community and faith— Surrounding world

There are numerous other elements one could include to describe fully a person's transcendent reference systems, for instance, tradition, a book, a piece of land, duty to family or kingdom, memories, revenge, service to others.

Each of these patterns of relationships places an individual's living in a transcendent context. Each of these systems of meaning may sustain the lives of some group of people. Each deals with the questions of ontology by defining several ways for humans to use their freedom to exercise control or are dependent and, therefore, trusting. Each defines how humans may balance the doing and being of living.

Chapter 8

Eschatology

Eschatology in my *American Heritage Dictionary of the English Language* is defined this way:

1. The branch of theology that is concerned with the end of the world or of humankind.
2. A belief or doctrine concerning the ultimate or final things, such as death, the destiny of humanity, or the Last Judgment.

Another dictionary I remember explained simply, the study of end things.

I think many people today are not concerned with the end of the world or the end of humanity. We are too involved in the present and have accepted a perspective of time derived from geology and astronomy. We think of the world as at least 10 billion years old and expect it to go on long after all of us are dead. We worried about atomic holocaust for a while, but that has faded into the back of our consciousness. Some of us know we are participating in an explosion of human population, but that does not pinch us too much just yet. The Last Judgment is a concept tied rather tightly to a limited range of Christianity. Eschatology does not seem to be relevant to us when approached in this way.

However, let me suggest that considering end things is a way of getting people to place the present and what they do in it within a transcendent context of time. The point that gives eschatology relevance and makes reflecting on it interesting is that human activity in the present has consequences in the future. All three soteriological responses to death depend on this connection for their significance.

If your faith says that there is life after death, what you do now—in this life—will presumably affect what happens then. Since this life is thought to be finite and the after life infinite, you should take this connection very seriously. If you believe in reincarnation, how you live this life is said to determine the conditions of your next life in the progression toward nirvana, which is the escape from eternal progression. If you believe that when you die, you are irretrievably dead and that is the end of you, you had better live life right the first and only time. Your only immortality is by what you did, how you did it, and how you will or will not be remembered by those who you influenced or affected. All of these religious scripts predict a future that transcends the present. They use this vision to mold and influence how we are to live in the present.

Eschatology considers end things: the end of the world, the end of all life forms, the end of 1,000 years, the end of each individual life, the end of this day, the end of the present moment. How are these endpoints connected? They all prompt us to ask, what can and should we do now to make ourselves comfortable with the anticipated endpoints in which we will participate? Our assumption is that the string of present moments we are passing through, during this life, will lead to some endpoint that we will either suffer or enjoy. Most religions use this transcending perspective to motivate individuals to use what they do with their solitariness for Good. The relevant religion and culture for any individual define that Good in each case.

To reflect upon how the present living of human beings is connected to the future is to focus upon two considerations:

1.   Time and change, and
2.   The choices we humans may have during our lifetime.

Time and Change

We humans know time through observing and experiencing change. We certainly measure time by the flicking of numbers on digital watches or as the hands move around the face of traditional watches. Few of us in secular society keep track of time by the movement of the sun or stars or moon anymore. We keep track of how much work we have done by how much time we have spent doing it. With the passing of time we grow older, more mature, and age, all the while moving from birth toward death. I submit this is the way the creativity of our Universe is immanent in and through us.

Our memory and imagination help us realize that nothing in our world has escaped change. There is nothing permanent or actually stable, even the rocks and the mountains and plains change slowly over time. Life is really living. Living is the passing from birth through childhood, adolescence, adulthood, old age (if we are lucky), and finally dying. To put it in experiential terms, living is growing out of dependence, learning to love and be (somewhat) independent with dignity, grieving for lost loves and things we cared for, suffering through illness and injury, recovering, planning, dreaming, doing, growing older, enjoying grandchildren, and dying. Therefore, to speak to what individuals do with their solitariness, any religion must conceive and consider a realistic and powerfully relevant understanding of time and change. Time and change are non-rational, demonstrable facts of our existence. With a reasonable and relevant understanding of time and change, a religion will have a long lasting and dramatic impact on the community of humans it serves.

Time and change constitute one of the transcendent reference systems within which we live. One of religion's tasks is to enable human beings to make sense or meaning of the events of living through which every individual comes to know that time is passing. "I am growing older," is a realization with power.

Our awareness of time and change comes as we are able to remember the past and then use our memories to imagine various futures. Our knowledge of time and change is improved when we compare our memories and imaginings with actual on-going experience. We live our lives in the instantaneous present. Only as we remember sequences of events do we connect what is past with the now. Only as we understand patterns and connections within the sequence that led to the present do we gain knowledge of cause and effect, repetition, coincidence, uniqueness, difference, and sameness. These examples are only to mention a few of the ways we organize our experiences of the world which are dependent on time and change.

Soteriology deals with how we humans go on living with the knowledge of our death. Death is the end of every human life. Ontology deals with what we are doing with our experiences of being and doing. Being and doing are how we move toward that end. The transcending reference system of time and change, **eschatology**, is an essential element for resolving both these and other concerns of theology.

Three fundamental images of time used by religions are linear, cyclical, and spiral in form. Each is rooted in experience, and uses memory and imagination. Each is both concrete and abstract. Each is both simple and complex. All three have delivered meaning to many generations of human lives:

> 1.   *Some understand time and change to be like a straight line.*
>   Every life moves from birth to death. This movement
>   passes through days which begin with dawn and end in
>   dusk, and nights which begin at sunset and end with
>   sunrise. Every year moves through seasons, yet no two
>   years are the same. Once a moment or day is gone, it can
>   never be called back. Although we may remember the
>   past, we cannot go back and change it. Through
>   forgetfulness and forgiveness, regrets and renewal, letting

go and resurrection, we may alter how the past limits our
future, but going back and reliving it is not an option.
Time and change from this perspective are linear.

The concepts of progress, fate, and destiny are dependent on this image
of time and change. When the metaphor of an line is used to understand
time, it is almost irresistible to ask where it is going. Where are we going?
Where am I going? What will be the end of my life? What will be the end
of time? How will I, we, be active in going there? These are questions
concerned with our future. In contrast we tend to accept the past as over
and done, to be accepted. These questions arise because we humans
experience everything in our world as having an end. We even measure
time in units, which have ends and beginnings: seconds, minutes, weeks,
years, centuries, millenniums. Why should not time also have an end?
Maybe time is truly infinite. However, our sense of *enough* still projects an
end in the far distant future.

Even secular thinking during the last 50 years has projected an
eschatological end. The world will end in nuclear holocaust, global
warming, by starvation after the human population explodes beyond the
supply of food and fresh water, by war, by social unrest after any or all of
the above. Therefore, we are told, "Do something now." If time is a line,
and we are progressing along it, and you do not like where you see us
going, then do something now to change the end state.

Eschatology is concerned with time and change, now and tomorrow,
means and ends. How will what we humans do today affect every end
toward which we are moving? How can we use fear of a projected or
prophesied end to change how people are living today?

2.   *Time is cyclical.* It runs in circles. As the seasons return in
      a never-ending rotation, as the planets circle the sky, as
      the sun and moon move in circles, as every life repeats
      the cycle from birth to death to rebirth of rearranged

molecules in new life forms, so life and time move in circles.

Faith in reincarnation gives living meaning with this image. The most powerful use of reincarnation comes from Asian religions. I have difficulty exploring this option because it is not grounded in the culture that has nourished and sustained me. However, the secular naturalist sees the material stuff of his physical body returning to the Universe as recyclable dust. "Out of the dust of stars we come," writes poet Kenneth Patton, "and to dust we shall return," adds the scriptures for Christian internment.

3.   *The third possibility suggests that time and change move in a spiral.* There is always a progression, even though we humans find ourselves revisiting experiences and questions about the meaning of living, not once but perhaps many times. In each culture every child goes through the same sequences of growth. Every healthy adult moves through the same stages of maturity, excepting cases of arrested development. Here there is a recognition that life is different for every person, for every generation it is different, yet it is the same. So there is a progression, but the movement is in overlapping circles.

All three images of the movement of time are drawn from experience. All three use memory and imagination to conceive patterns, which are orderly. All three seek to know the patterns from the past so that the future may be anticipated and predicted, influenced, or controlled. Success in the discipline of eschatology leads to knowledge and wisdom, and some power to choose the events that will make up our lives and the meaning we will give each.

Reality and Grace

Two contrasting understandings of time and change are significant for eschatology in our secular culture. They also present us with one of the major ways the secular view of reality and the religious view of reality differ. In short, our secular view of the world speaks of cause and effect, while religion says grace is an essential reality of human living.

Cause-and-effect so permeates our secular living and understanding of the modern world that it does not need further explanation. The sciences have focused on the material world, measuring inputs and results, and been stupendously successful. I honor and celebrate this success upon which our modern world depends.

The purpose of science and the technology that follows from it is to give us the ability to predict and control the events of our living and world. Science seeks out independent and dependent variables, and then conducts experiments to learn how they are related. When we know what the dependent variables are, we may manipulate the independent variables to make accurate predictions and exercise control of future events. The ability of science and technology to do this is expanding into ever more areas of human concern. To know and control the relationship between dependent and independent variables is to control cause and effect.

Is our human experience of time and change adequately covered by the idea of cause-and-effect? If all the world is governed by cause and effect, why do we have undeniable experiences of chance and freedom of choice? Even physical sciences contain the realities of the uncertainty principle, chaos, and probability theory which may be used to account for chance in an otherwise well-ordered world. Also, it is now acceptable in secular conversation to speak of serendipity and coincidence because even scientists do so. In more casual conversation, we speak of good luck and bad luck. There are events in our living that we did not control or anticipate which truly may be uncontrollable. These are events we must accept and live with as facts that are part of our past.

Does this understanding of time and change, based on cause and effect but with occasional luck or serendipity thrown in, adequately and coherently account for our human experience of the reality in which we live? I suggest that it does not. After years of living within this secular worldview with discomfort, I now live within and understand our world with a perspective that includes grace as a major category of perception. This inclusion of grace is essential to understanding the function of religion in human living.

Now what do I mean by **grace**? I believe that the fundamental experience that underlies all meanings of grace is the exquisite timing of many events in our living. These are events we did not anticipate, predict, or control through cause and effect. After the fact we may be able to trace a sequence of cause and effect leading to the event in question, however there still is an element of exquisite timing. This timing brings both good and ill, benedictions and maledictions, into our lives.

Let me tell a story to illustrate. Years ago I visited an ailing and recent member of the church I was serving in Arkansas. His first question to me when I entered his nursing home room was, "Oh, so you are a preacher. What do you do with Job?" Dying of throat cancer, he was sitting on a metal folding chair. Job sat before me and wanted to know what kind of a preacher/pastor I was. That day I had no answer to his question. This was good enough for him. I continued our visits, and became his friend and pastor. Eventually I was asked to do his funeral and interment services.

Some months later on the day of his funeral, the sky over Arkansas was dark with clouds and rain. It rained all during the morning of my 80-mile drive to the small town in the delta where he was to be buried. Although the rain stopped as I entered the town, the clouds still completely covered the heavens. I read the funeral service. I suspect that he and I were the only Unitarians in the room. His family was Southern Baptist. I was conscious of the tension between my religious faith and theirs. I made what was probably an unsuccessful attempt to bridge this distance. We all drove a half mile to the country cemetery at the conclusion of the service.

As we drove into the cemetery, the heavens opened and beams of sunlight streamed through to illuminate his grave and burial gathering. The graveside service took only minutes before the heavens closed and rain began again. It was a perfectly natural event, there was nothing supernatural about it, BUT THE TIMING WAS EXQUISITE. Is it too much to say that the heavens opened to receive that old man's spirit? Many in his family considered him an unrepentant heretic and probably missed the opening of the heavens. It was a miracle if one had the eyes to see and a heart to understand, if one accepted the facts. This event obeyed all the laws of nature. It was exquisite timing. It was grace.

On the drive home I reflected on how exquisite timing permeates my living, all our lives. Each one of us is born, and born with certain genes. Every adult I know has survived numerous close calls in accidents. What about how we met the significant others in our lives? I thought of the many events in the Old Testament, which have exquisite timing as their essence and are named the work of God. For instance, in the Exodus when the Hebrews are trapped against the Reed Sea and Moses prays, the waters part, letting the former slaves escape. Even today the wind is known to blow across the desert sands and push the water of the Reed Sea to one side. If this was a perfectly natural event that happened to Moses and his people, we are still confronted with its exquisite timing just when the Hebrews needed it.

I thought of how exquisite timing has benefited me and also added to the burdens to my living. I now understand exquisite timing to be the essence of grace. "The work of God is known through grace," is a saying that now makes sense to me in a way it never did before.

Human Choices

Many in our secular world dismiss the timing of events as luck and think no more about it. However, if anyone chooses to do something with his or her solitariness, if anyone seeks to know and accept the meaning of human living, then exquisite timing, as an element of the reality that has given us life and is present in every moment, cannot be excluded or ignored. Both cause and effect and exquisite timing are part of the reality in which we humans live.

Some people do not and cannot experience this dimension of reality, which I am naming exquisite timing. I know this to be so, but I do not fully understand why it is so. The reality of exquisite timing invites human beings to construct or conceive or create some interpretation for it. I believe that one way human beings come to know God is by reflecting on the grace in their living. There is a correlation in the people I know between those who do not experience grace and those who are atheists or agnostics. I recognize them as humanists. I do not believe or conclude that to know grace is to know God. That conclusion is not a necessity. It is only one conclusion of many that are possible.

It is true that if one fully acknowledges and reflects upon grace, then a new transcendent dimension of reality opens and must be included in one's understanding of self as a participant embedded in the creativity of our Universe. The process of on-going time and change that one must live with is known to be transcendent in a way that is not and will never be fully controllable. Nevertheless, the question for living fully remains, how will I respond to this fact of reality?

How will each of us respond to grace, to the exquisite timing of the events in our living? Will we reach for control and build our lives expecting to be in control? Will we respond with confusion or frustration or anger or rage or depression, when we are not in control? Will we work ourselves to despair and death from the not so pure joy of using the control we do have? Will we reach for power and control over other individuals and communities? How will we use the power and control we as superpower Americans have? How will any of us use the power and influence we have by virtue of the political or corporate office we hold? How will parents, teachers, physicians use the knowledge and power they have? Will we use power and control as if we earned it or deserved it more than someone else? Will we act as if we owned the material things in our lives? Will we use our power and wealth to further justice for all? Will we use it for the benefit of ourselves and the transcendent human community? Will we use our power with an appropriate sense of reverence, with a dynamic sense of perspective and proportion? Will we know and respond to appropriate limits? Will we act appropriately when enough is enough?

One of the primary experiences that follows from knowing grace as part of the reality in which you live is helplessness. Helplessness does not imply powerlessness or that you are without choices. **Helplessness** means that you are not in full control. In every situation we are more or less in control. We may learn what to do to remove obstacles which keep the good from happening. We may also know many things that will enable good to happen and choose to do them, but in the final analysis, we must trust and let the good we seek happen.

I once was called to serve a congregation where I realized that their worship space had been created 28 years before my arrival and had not been redecorated since. It looked shabby to me. It also was well used and much loved by all the members of the congregation. They were very comfortable using it. Their comfort was an obstacle to change. As a newcomer, I could not be too critical. So I told them how well used and much loved the room appeared to me. After three weeks someone asked me what I was saying. I pointed out the holes in the carpet, the dirty shadows above the heat vents, the battered appearance of the wood of the stage. I asked if any of the women present had let their living room go 25 years without rearrangement or redecorating? The members began to see what I saw. And then, in time, the congregation became uncomfortable with the situation. They asked, what could be done? I replied that we could appoint a committee to come up with a comprehensive plan to redecorate the room. It took three years and some $250,000 for the church to acquire a very different feel and personality with its renovated space. I removed some obstacles to set a process in motion and then had to wait for the Good to happen.

How will human beings respond to grace? Some do not experience it. Some ignore and repress the knowledge of it. Some respond with grief, frustration, anger, rage, terrorism, insanity. Some respond with confusion. Some respond with acceptance and then faith, hope, and trust. Some respond with thanksgiving, wonder and awe, reverence. Some respond with curiosity, imagination, reflection, myths, stories, and interpretations, and some with prayers for blessings or acceptance of the unacceptable.

The value of eschatology is how it draws our attention to the way time and change permeate our living. Eschatology asks us to reflect upon the relationship of every potential future to the present we are now living. Eschatology asks, how will human beings respond? What will you do with your solitariness.

Chapter 9

Metaphysics

In my third edition of the *American Heritage Dictionary...*, metaphysics is defined as, "The branch of philosophy that examines the nature of reality, including the relationship between mind and matter, substance and attribute, fact and value." I will use **metaphysics** to mean the branch of theology that considers the nature of reality. I do not know a branch of theology that names the concerns I wish to raise here.

In the past 25 years metaphysics has been held in some disrepute by many in our secular society. It has not been a subject for general discussion. So some will be asking, why do you raise these issues here? It is necessary to include metaphysics in functional theology because I expect all religions to be realistic. Not only do we need to understand and appreciate what it means to be realistic, we need to distinguish between the meanings of "rational" and "realistic." We need to have both permission and the means to discuss what reality is and what it is not. We need a means that enables us to critique the various interpretations of reality that inform individuals as well as religions.

Some concerns can be gathered under no other label. Fundamental to the understanding of this approach to religion is the complexity of our world and the reality surrounding each individual human and whole communities of individuals. Each religious person selects and responds to some of the transcendent elements of this complexity, and then interprets those selected entities. We may fully understand and appreciate a given religious faith only if we name the concerns and questions that flow from asking whether this selected reality is adequate and applicable, and maintained with appropriate perspective and proportion.

If, as secular culture tends to do, we do not appropriately separate what it means to use reason from what it means to be realistic and reverent, then we make thinking and understanding religion in our modern world ever so much more confusing, if not impossible. There is a difference between being realistic and being rational. And responding to life with reverence adds a much-needed perspective to how we humans are rational and realistic.

Within the functional understandings I am proposing here, to be **rational** means to be consistent and coherent in one's thinking. In contrast, to be **realistic** means to be adequate and applicable in the way you understand and relate to the surrounding world of entities, things, and relationships. To be **reverent** means to bring an active sense of transcendent perspective and proportion to how you respond to living.

Isn't it unfortunate that the form of reverence most frequently used is a noun to identify clergy when it could be used as a verb that is essential to allow human beings to do something worthwhile with their solitariness? It seems to me that there is a distinction to be recognized between the metaphysics of materialism and the metaphysics with which religions are concerned. Materialism is primarily concerned with things that can be measured or known through our five senses. Materialism names, categorizes, and organizes our physical world so we can learn how to predict and control it. Religion, on the other hand, is concerned with how human beings use transcendent systems of meaning to do something with their experience of solitariness. Religions give us a response to the pattern of exquisite timing in the events of our living, which I name the essence of Grace. Our human sense of transcendence is essential to religion and defines the reality with which religion is concerned.

I believe there is truth in saying that much of materialism concerns the use of reason to seek the simplest and smallest in order to gain control and allow prediction. Reverence should not be left out in this process, but is frequently much ignored. Religion uses reverence to seek the ultimate transcendent humans may know in our world. The goals sought by all religions are acceptance and spiritual health. Reason is always actively present in theological reflection, yet expresses itself very differently here from the way it is used in materialism. Within theology and materialism both reason and reverence are present, yet the goal sought and results achieved are very different.

In our world of global communication and economics, the major traditional world religions are living in tension with each other in ways they have not before. I know of mosques in Ohio and Michigan, Buddhist monks in Lincoln, Nebraska, and Christian missionaries in communities all over the world. The divisions within each major religion are becoming more and more obvious and, in some cases, in tension with each other. Witness the growing distance and tension between fundamentalist and more moderate followers of all religious traditions.

How are we to account for these differences? Yes, the differences are based on differing interpretations of scripture in some cases, and differing visions of living in others. All live in a single transcendent reality and yet choose very different transcendent systems of reference and values upon which to base the meaning of their religion and living. Sometimes the differences seem small to outsiders, yet wars have been fought over these differences. Each then proceeds to be rational within its understanding of reality. There is always a tendency to act as if "ours" is the only reality that will give fulfilling meaning to living.

The issues I raise here have wider applications than religion. In recent years there has been a growing awareness of the difference between the realities that are natural to males and females. Again both are rational within the reality they know and use. These realities are revealed in the subtle differences in how males and females use words and the expectations they bring to relationships. Some people are now able to shift their use of language and perception between male and female realities.

Also, we often speak of the values held by separate ethnic, national, or cultural communities. Many of these differences have to do with how each community experiences the reality of our world. I am suggesting that ethnic differences include value choices, how reason is used, and an understanding of reality that is primary to the identity of that ethnic community. Every ethnic community uses a particular perspective and sense of proportion in shaping its identify and traditions. Every ethnic community is rational within its understanding of reality. Each uses reverence to organize and integrate the *transcending reference systems of meaning* which surround its members as human beings. Each seeks to live consistently within the worldview and tradition so established. To know oneself as a black American is very different from knowing oneself as a white American. Each incorporates skin color as symbolic of ethnic identity, which carries significant meaning and implications for the individual's identity and community membership. Knowledge of Spanish or some other ethnic heritage one accepts may fulfill a similar function. Ethnic identity carries a complex set of values and understandings, which define what it means to be realistic within that community. Within this reality one then lives rationally, with consistency and coherence.

One of the most striking arguments for naming metaphysics as an important concern is that our human intellectual freedom depends in large measure on our ability to shift metaphysics. Every person has a most comfortable understanding of reality, which feels like home. To relate to other people, we shift our home reality ever so slightly to include theirs if they are friends or companions. Observable differences ask us to consider larger shifts of inclusion. Every language has a perspective of reality. If two people are to understand each other when using two different languages, they must be able to shift from one perspective to the other.

Intellectual freedom ultimately depends upon one's ability to shift in these ways:

- Recognize the difference between two or more realities human beings live in

- Accept each as valid and functional
- Temporarily think and act "as if" either is true
- Consciously use the one needed to function in a given situation

If we are to have peace in the world between national, religious, and ethnic communities, we must learn how to accept and live with different ways humans know the reality of our Universe. We must accept that being a secular American who believes in democracy and capitalism is not the only way to be a good human being. One may be Christian, Moslem, Hindu, Buddhist, or Humanist and, in all cases, be a good human being. One may be European, Chinese, Japanese, or Indian and, likewise, be a good human being. Every nation has its own form of government and economic organization. These religious and nationalistic labels gain meaning as each defines a portion of reality for the members of its community.

Let me acknowledge here that to raise metaphysical issues in this way involves us in paradox. There is only one transcendent reality within which all human beings live. Yet there are many ways we humans know it and live within it. All are simultaneously true, and have been functional for many generations. Each responds to our human condition bringing vitality and vibrance, faith and meaning, to some community of human beings. Is not this the essence of paradox?

With this much said, let us accept that metaphysics (what is real) is important enough to be included here and ask, why are there differences in the realities religions deal with? In short, I do not know. I take it as a fact that I observe.

Even though I don't know the answer, I do have a response in the form of this metaphor. Why do some people like classical music and others country, jazz, pop, or rock? They do, and these differences may reflect fundamental difference in life style. However, the differences are non-threatening. Some of the factors that influence a person's preference in music are genes, family background, education, natural gifts in music, life style and pace, ethnic heritage, national identity. These are the same factors, I suggest, that govern which religion makes sense to us.

Let us also note that there is a very wide variety of ability in music. Some individuals just listen, others play an instrument, some sing, others compose, and a few conduct bands and orchestras. Some can do several of these things. Genetic gifts, education, skill, dedication, discipline, years of practice and involvement are some of the factors that determine a person's current musical ability. We give appropriate deference to those who are gifted, skilled, and experienced in music.

We should bring the same expectations and deference to matters religious because in matters of religion the same factors apply. Some individuals have ignored religious concerns for years. Others have paid attention when a death intruded in their busy living. Others have participated in a religious community all their lives. Some have sought out training and/or spent years pursuing religious concerns. We should expect different capacities for experiencing and different levels of insight, knowledge, and wisdom from each of these people.

So why are there different religions? Why do different people hold different religious faiths? Why does the depth of religious understanding vary so much within any given community? Well, the facts are simply that there are different religions, and different people do hold different religious faiths, and there is a great diversity of faith communities and much variety within each one. The task we are working on is, how shall we respond to this situation? Can we formulate a functional understanding of religion, which will do four things?

- Give us understanding of each as viable and pragmatic
- Ask questions that all respond to in one way or another
- Enable us to compare and contrast them
- Enable followers of one to talk meaningfully to members of another

A functional way to answer these four questions is to investigate how each religion is realistic and relevant, and uses reason and reverence. Remember, this is to ask every religion to be adequate and applicable, coherent and consistent, and maintain a vital and vibrant perspective and sense of proportion. It is also to accept that no one religion has the only absolute truth for our human condition, yet every one has been or is appropriately relevant to a particular community of human beings.

Functional religious metaphysics asks, what gives definition and clarity to the reality within which individuals are doing something with their solitariness? Which transcending reference systems of meaning are used to respond to living, dying, change, creativity?

Reality and Webs of Meaning

At the center of our concern are individuals and what they are doing with their solitariness. There are several ways to respond to the reality of every human individual. All are simultaneously true. It depends on how one chooses to look at or approach the subject, the condition of being human. This is a paradox. If we restrict ourselves to the material aspects of our humanity, we may consider the atomic or molecular or cellular reality; or, we may consider the chemical, electrical, or organic reality of any individual. If we enter the social dimension of our human condition, we may consider the psychological, political, economic, or social realities within which human beings live and in which they participate. Within our secular world of knowledge, we expect every one of these disciplined ways of studying our human condition to be both rational and empirical. There is of course another human activity which is not covered by any of the above mentioned ways of knowing. That is religion. I expect it to be also both rational and empirical. I add one more layer to the paradoxical mix that is needed to adequately and coherently understand what it means to be fully human.

The basic task of religion is to enable human beings to know, accept, and celebrate the meaning of their solitariness as they are a part of and dependent upon communities of other humans and living organisms, and experience the creativity of our Universe moving them toward death. I suggest an image of our human condition, which involves a paradox. It is true that every individual is a separate and discrete entity. Each of us exists within our own skins. And it is also true that each of us is the center of a web of relationships. Our sanity, health, and the meaning of our living depend on this web of relatedness. This web is like a spider's web that has a center space and concentric circles around the center ring. There are arms or threads reaching out from the center ring through the surrounding circles to find anchor points somewhere out beyond the center circle. These arms or threads connect the rings and hold the matrix of our relationships in an ordered pattern.

For purposes of functional religious reflection I think of each person as such a web. Each person is the space in the middle. Without the surrounding pattern, the person lacks identity. Every web is unique, yet all have some common aspects. Each radius, connecting point, and circle represents an event, an understanding, a person, and a relationship that is part of the meaning of our living. When someone whom we care about dies, a significant part of the web of meaning that has been our self is torn away. The closer the person is to us, the more the integrity of the inner circle is threatened or even violated. **Grief** is the process of learning to create a new pattern for our web.

There are rings, segments, points of connection, and radiating arms in every web of meaning. There are also degrees of concreteness and abstraction, distance from the self and positions of importance. In just one day of living, a person will focus on or use different portions of the web depending on the circumstances and activity that are relevant at the moment. For some concerns the set of the rings in a person's web of meaning will be used as a nested whole, with each larger ring including and dependent upon those inside it. However, in other circumstances, the rings of the web may appear to change in proximity to the center.

This functional understanding of religion suggests that every individual creates a web of meaning as they grow through childhood and into maturity. As adults we strive to maintain the continuity of relationships which make up the web of our living. We strive to accept and adjust to the on-going changes both within ourselves and to the external environment. Each ring is larger than the ones inside, closer to the center, surrounding the center of the web with transcendent or transcending rings of reference and meaning. The radiating threads reach out seeking points of reference until it is enough for that person whose life is the center of the web. There is a sense in which each ring includes and transcends all that is inside of it. Religion's concern is to define and sustain the anchor points sustaining the pattern of the web, and then to nurture an ultimate and most inclusive ring of meaning.

Reality and Spiritual Health

Religion's task is to enable us to sustain and enhance the complexity of the meaning web that sustains our human spiritual health. **Spiritual health** is the way the web of meaning that surrounds every individual sustains his or her vitality and vibrance of living. Spiritual health concerns how the transcendent reference systems of meaning are known, accepted, and integrated into an organic whole. That whole is realistic, relevant, rational, and reverent of the creation and creativity within which the individual lives.

I have been a Unitarian Universalist minister since finishing theological school and have had the opportunity to serve several liberal religious congregations. None has sustained its identity by the use of a creed. Each has been a religious community gathered to explore and celebrate the religious meaning of the lives of those who choose to join. All have affirmed the ability of individuals living within our secular culture to do something appropriate and dynamic with their solitariness. These years of ministry have given me a rather unusual opportunity to listen and observe how both male and female human beings struggle for spiritual health. I have participated as they have coped with love and grief, despair and hope, joy and sorrow, living and dying. Together we have celebrated births and deaths, weddings and birthdays, holidays and Holy Days.

The confusion of serving as minister in such an open community was overwhelming at first. Gradually I began to realize that I was hearing only four ways of weaving religious meaning in our secular world. Every one of my congregants was rational and realistic in as many as four different ways. Each way was reverent with a difference. All held many aspects of the transcendent reality in common. Yet, each used a different transcendent reference from which the meaning of living was understood and from which guiding values were derived.

The four ways of relating to reality with spiritual health are expressed in what I call the Four Faiths: humanism, naturalism, mysticism, and theism. Several options or variations occur within each of them. However, some patterns of meaning overlap so that all individuals within each of the Four Faiths share them. I have been able to distinguish the Four Faiths from one another because each uses our common English language differently. The same words are spoken, but the meaning intended for key words shifts. First, let me define each of the Four Faiths in general terms. Then I will discuss briefly some metaphysical concerns and questions.

- **Humanists** use the human community as the primary transcendent reference system of meaning for the content of their religion. Science is much trusted.

- **Naturalists** understand themselves as participants in and dependent upon the natural world as the transcendent reference system of meaning within which they find their religious identity. The natural world includes all living organisms on our globe and all elements of our Universe.

This faith also strongly trusts the sciences for knowledge of the world and to describe reality.

- **Mystics** have had an experience of "union with the transcendent," or other experiences which they know the sciences exclude. These experiences are so strong or occur frequently enough that they cannot be denied. Mystics draw the meaning of life and the values that shape their living from the experience of the relationship and union with the transcendent they know in their solitariness.

- **Theists** have experience of a presence, which is known as a "THOU," named God. Any theist tradition which has served to bring meaning to human living over many generations will have layers and layers of meaning and interpretation about the being or concept of God. Each generation has added to what the previous ones have revealed. God, for theists, points to a transcendent flowing pattern of events that individuals trust and know themselves to be profoundly dependent upon. Trust and dependence are known from direct experience.

There are several variations within each of these four major faiths. I have found that those individuals who claim to follow any given one of them share a common sense of reality and use language in common ways. If a person from one faith is visiting with people of another, very likely all will feel tension in the way they understand key words. By hearing this difference in the use of language, I first distinguished the four as separate.

To illustrate how subtle, yet profound, metaphysical differences are, here is an exercise for an adult religious education course I created and led called "Four Faiths." I developed a questionnaire (see pages 97) in an effort to dramatize the different realities that each of the four faiths depend on and to show a way in which they hold the same perceptions of reality. Tabulated results follow reproduction of the questionnaire.

These instructions were given with questionnaire:

> Use the scales below to indicate how important each side
> of the polarity created by two ideas is as an element in
> the reality you live in. Use one circle on each scale unless
> you feel the extremes are so balanced that you need to
> circle 1 and 5. In this case think of the line as a circle,
> then 1 and 5 are next to each other not at extreme ends.

I included the 1/ 5 option because when I shifted my mind to operate within the reality of a mystic, I realized that marking 3 to express a balance between the two extremes does not appropriately reflect a mystic's position. The defining fact for mystics is a union of self and the transcendent. Since this is so, then 1 and 5 are not at opposite ends of a line, but next to each other as if the numbers are around a circle. I interpreted the choice of both 1 and 5 as a 6. The results (page 98) confirm that my guess was correct.

The questionnaire was not refined and the resulting average composition of participants comes from only one group of 75 people. Of the 75 people about 10% identified themselves as theists, 15 % humanist, 25 % mystics, and about 50 % naturalists. I find the results suggestive, not necessarily valid scientifically, yet very illuminating.

The complete chart on page 92 presents the simple averages of the choices given by a Four Faiths workshop. I averaged the numerical choices made by the people in each group. Please note the first four items were conceived to define each of the four faiths and the scores reflect the identity of the faith named. The differences in the scores illustrate the width of separation between them. Items 5, 11, 12, 14 (Control—Trust, Family—Service, Problem solving—Relationship, and Possessions—People) suggest values held in common. Items 6, 10, 15 (Order—Chaos, Self—Work/Cause, and Being me—Fitting in) suggest a much wider spread of values between the four faiths. The rest of the scores show that some aspects of reality are shared and some of the four faiths may differ from the others in a particular case.

Four Faiths Questionnaire

1. Self   Human Community

    1   2   3   4   5

2. Self   Natural World

    1   2   3   4   5

3. Self   Mystic Union

    1   2   3   4   5

4. Self   God

    1   2   3   4   5

5. Control   Trust

    1   2   3   4   5

6. Order   Chaos

    1   2   3   4   5

7. Product   Process

    1   2   3   4   5

8. Works   Faith

    1   2   3   4   5

9. Self   Transcendence

    1   2   3   4   5

10. Self   Work or Cause

    1   2   3   4   5

11. Family   Community Service

    1   2   3   4   5

12. Problem   Solving Relationship

    1   2   3   4   5

13. My Self-worth   Community
Involvement

    1   2   3   4   5

14. Possessions (mine)   People (relationships)

    1   2   3   4   5

15. Being Me   Fitting in a Larger
Pattern
1   2   3   4   5

Four Faiths Questionnaire: Results

Continuum	Humanist	Naturalist	Mystic	Theist
1. Self—Human Community	5.5	4.4	4.1	3.4
2. Self—Natural World	3.2	4.7	4.4	4.1
3. Self—Mystic Union	1.9	1.4	5.8	4.2
4. Self—God	1.7	1.2	3.8	6.0
5. Control—Trust	3.8	3.6	3.8	4.8
6. Order—Chaos	1.7	2.4	4.0	2.7
7. Product—Process	3.8	3.5	5.1	4.8
8. Works—Faith	2.5	1.7	3.6	3.8
9. Self—Transcendence	3.1	2.8	4.8	4.2
10. Self—Work/Cause	5.0	4.1	4.4	3.3
11. Family—Service	3.6	3.4	3.6	2.7
12. Problem Solving—Relationship	3.9	3.8	4.0	3.6
13. Self-worth —Community Involvement	4.6	3.3	4.8	3.0
14. Possessions—People	4.8	4.1	4.4	4.6
15. Being Me —Fitting in a Larger pattern	2.2	2.5	5.0	3.0

When I was younger I described myself as a humanist and agnostic. However, religious questions would not let me rest. As my awareness of our Universe's creativity and grace has increased in depth and appreciation, I have come to accept God as one way to relate to and understand the inclusive transcendent reference system in which I live. I now understand that the way a person experiences and interprets change and grace determines whether they will know God as part of their religious reality. There are other ways to come to know God; however, this is one. I describe myself now as a naturalistic mystic.

Over the last eight years of my chosen career I was an interim minister, moving every year or two to work with a new congregation in transition. During these years I led groups of adults in six different cities, using functional definitions of key religious words and inviting the participants to accept one of the four faiths as their own. The purpose of the course was to give permission and enable individuals to own and accept what they were doing with their solitariness. We explored during eight sessions what each person had done, was doing, with their solitariness. Each session posed a question drawn from one of the areas of theological concern included in this essay and invited discussion of the possible answers suggested by functional theology. From 50 to 100 people in each of six congregations participated in the course, so I have some empirical confirmation that the functional definitions and Four Faiths are applicable in the real world of our secular society. The enthusiasm and interest in the course and its ideas validate the crisis of religious integrity in our secular culture. This functional way of understanding religion responds to this crisis with clarity and power.

I introduce these four faiths here because I do not consider myself a scholar of world religions and am only an observer of Christianity and Judaism. I believe that using some relatively concrete examples of how differing religious faiths create the web of realistic meaning within which they enable individuals to respond to solitariness will make our discussion of metaphysics more easily understood. I will leave it to my readers to apply the functional definitions to the religious tradition with which they are most concerned. By using more generic faiths, I slight all and none.

Metaphysics and Theology

I use metaphysics in a descriptive, not a prescriptive way. I am concerned with the reality that people actually relate to and not about the one someone thinks they should or ought to relate to. I am making a distinction between "what is" and "what I want or wish." I also expect every perception of reality we will discuss or mention to be derived from someone's experience.

Implications of this statement affect people uniquely and personally. If one has not had the experiences that lead human beings to know a given aspect of reality, then that aspect of reality will not be included in the religious understanding of that person. Every person constructs the reality within which his or her religion functions on the basis of direct personal experience or upon interpretations of experience given by companions he trusts. If the religious meaning informing the community of which one is a member is at variance with one's personal experience, then a problem of integrity presents itself. Let me explain this a bit more.

When I was writing of soteriology, I suggested that there are three possible answers to the question, what do you believe happens at the death of a human being?

1.   There is some form of being after death ("life after death").
2.   When people die, they are dead. There is nothing of any consequence left.
3.   I believe we humans are reincarnated into another life after this life is over.

Each answer reaches into a transcendent realm to give living in the present meaning, to enable individuals to live with vitality in spite of the knowledge of death. The reality of what each describes is very different. Each of these answers is based on faith and experience.

Christianity is an example of a faith in life after death. An experience and reflection which may lead to this conclusion is that death ending human life is simply unacceptable. Or, there is life after death because people of authority and wisdom say it is so. Life after death does not have to be connected to the beliefs in heaven and hell. However, if it is, then there is accountability in the form of justice for evil people and reward for good people who suffer in this life. Life after death may be understood to be physical or spiritual. Each option adds another element to the reality within which this faith operates.

Hinduism offers an example of belief in reincarnation. I am not a scholar of Hinduism, however I submit that this is a religion that has made sense and brought religious meaning to many generations of people. Reincarnation is based on the powerful and fundamental circular repetition human beings experience in the movement of the stars and planets, the seasons, the stages of life.

That human living ends in death also finds a transcendent reference in the Theory of Evolution, which says we human beings are animals and like all other life forms we die. We give our lives one day at a time, procreate, and die. Life goes on. Living has meaning; every life has meaning as it contributes to this eternal process. This is the faith of many humanists and naturalists.

Over the course of the last several years I have found that all three answers to death may be held as true by someone in each of the Four Faiths. However, life after death and reincarnation tend to be preferred by mystics and theists, while naturalists and humanists prefer the finality of "when you die, you are dead."

To discuss the metaphysical issues that follow from or are latent within ontology, we must accept that each person's needs, emotions, feelings, opinions, values held, history, hurts and scars remembered and forgotten, are who they are. All these things are real for each of us. They determine what perspective and sense of proportion each of us brings to the balance we sustain between being and doing. As we grow older, more mature, and age, we tend to shift the weight of the values shaping our living from doing to being. The meaning of every human life is defined by the balance between being and doing they maintain in their living. Another shift in the perception of reality that occurs as one ages is from expecting to be in control of things to accepting events as they come. Some would describe this as adjusting to the condition of being human. Youth tend to rebel and act as if they are immortal. One mark of maturity is the level of acceptance of those things that are beyond our control.

If I am to realistically relate to you, I must accept you as who you are now. I must seek to discover what parts of your web of meaning are congruent with mine or how they resonate with each other. If we have shared experiences and history, then the bond between us will be more easily formed and stronger.

Remember that we are discussing the religious crisis of integrity within our secular society. To say this is to accept that there is a secular understanding and set of values that tend to dominate our world and the way we live. The short name for it is materialism. One way to understand religion in this setting is to say that religion functions to maintain the spiritual health of individuals by placing each within a series of transcendent reference systems of meaning. These are not material entities, yet many are made up of material things. Religion nevertheless accepts transcendent reference systems of meaning as real. So the task of theological metaphysics is to study the patterns of transcendent reference systems of meaning that each religion uses as it sustains the meaning and spiritual health of the individuals and communities it serves.

After thinking about the metaphysics of religion in this way for some time, I have found that there are several general patterns that will help our reflection and understanding. These are patterns that tend to separate each religious faith from all the others. First let me list some of the patterns I have discovered:

1. Self—community—sacred tradition—God
2. Self—human community—community of living things—the natural physical world—ideas—the creativity of our Universe
3. Self—community—a religious tradition—the secular world—God
4. Self—family—work—corporation or cause—pleasure

5. Self—family—science—teaching—fame
6. Self—family —working a piece of land—church—
community—nation

I derived these lists from my observations of how many people in our American secular society seem to be living. To me, these patterns of values do describe different life styles in our society. I am sure each of us will conclude that some of these patterns bring greater satisfaction and fulfillment to human living than others. To reach that conclusion is one of the benefits of thinking about the metaphysics of religion.

Here is a series of questions involving pairs of entities or concepts drawn from my experience as a minister. These pairs work in a polarity with each other. Each end has more or less reality in relation to its partner. This list is intended to be suggestive and not exhaustive of the possible items that might be included. The distance between the paired items is a reflection of reality being defined in different ways.

1. Is time linear or does it run in circles?
2. What is the context of life in terms of process: cause and effect or grace?
3. Is the reality of our world order or chaos?
4. What is the balance between individual identity and the needs of the community?
5. Is sin or suffering understood to be the central problem of human living?
6. How are material things and consciousness understood? Which is the central reality of humanity?
7. Is the human body or soul the primary concern of health?
8. Which has more force in giving life meaning: a tradition of knowledge and wisdom or the experience of this generation?

The following questions raise the same issues. In this list I have included some items that distinguish certain religions from others, and some distinguish religious from secular reality. What and why is one interpretation of reality accepted and another not?

1.   What authorities are given power to set forth the truth about living: clergy, teachers, parents, scientists, books, experience?

2.   What experiences of transcendent reference systems and the world of things are determinative for the individual and community?

3.   What are the definitions of non-sense, false, or non-functional beliefs versus The Truth?

4.   What ideas are labeled as outside our beliefs, as superstitious and heretical? And why are they so treated?

5.   How does an individual and the community he or she lives in deal with history and tradition?

6.   How are rituals and symbols used to dramatize the meaning of life?

7.   How are emotions, passions, and faith used to sustain order and purpose in living?

As we humans seek to live within and sustain community with people who have found the meaning of their lives in different religious traditions and different national or linguistic groups, we need to separate how each is and has been realistic and rational. It seems to me that all people strive to be consistent in the way they live their values and live within their understanding of reality. It is true that every human has the ability to be confused, acting toward one value that is in tension or contradiction with another. This is to get into issues of ethics, which is the subject of the next chapter. For now let me point out that the values a person holds, which motivate him or her to act, are part of that person's reality. Just because they differ from values you or I accept, does not mean they are irrational. They are part of the non-rational identity of that person.

Chapter 10

Ethics

I understand ethics to be the study of values and how human beings use them. In some dictionaries ethics is defined as the study of morals or the principles of right conduct. I will use a broader understanding here in order to clarify the meaning of morality as sets of values, which have a special characteristic. **Ethics**, as I will use it, means the study of our human use of values. **Values** are anything, including an entity, toward which human beings have expended or will expend effort, time, or wealth. **Moral values** are those sets of values which a person or community expects to be applied or followed with consistency. I will discuss in some detail moral values later.

Values

Values are expressed in both words and actions. Any person or group is capable of putting one set of values into speech and living another, saying one thing and doing something else. When these two levels of our being are in agreement we humans are said to have integrity. If another person notices the lack of agreement, he or she will have a problem trusting us. The ways in which any community's speech and action are inconsistent or incoherent with each other reveals much about the real identity of the group and who has power in it.

Most values are non-rational. Values that are accepted and affirmed by a person are facts. They shape a person's living and the living of the community of which that person is a member. One may not like or approve of the values another person acts upon or lives by. One may judge some values as not leading to happiness or health or to the good of the person or his community. One may visit another culture or ethnic group and just not understand why the people are doing what they are doing. We tend to think of our own values as things we have chosen, as an expression of our freedom. However, for all peoples some values have been held and followed so long that they become part of the governing reality. They are no longer questioned and no longer are matters of choice.

A set of values defines a culture or ethnic group, and individuals within the group accept a particular set as part of their identity. The group members may be willing to expend much effort and wealth, or even fight to defend the values defining their group. The goal is to insure the values-as-a-set survive and are passed on to the next generation. Values are inherited by individuals from the family they are born into (or from the people with whom they spend their formative years) and through the daily and formal education they receive while growing toward maturity. If an individual lives in a setting in which there is never an alternative set of values experienced, then the inherited ethnic or peer values are constant and defining. They may slowly change over long periods of time, but generally they are not values individuals may exercise choice about.

If a member of one in-group confronts someone from another ethnic way of being human or with a different way of religion, then the values of ethnic identity may be questioned and become open to choice.

Speaking in rather general terms, I believe that maintaining ethnic identity is getting more difficult in some nations of our globe. Before World War II in America, we read about other peoples and occasionally someone from a foreign land came to visit, but most children experienced the values of other ethnic groups or peoples from foreign lands with only passing interest. If different value sets were present, they tended to be segregated. Now almost every town has several ethnic identity groups—white, Latino, black—and each with several subgroups. Also there are major religious groups in many of our cities—Catholic, Protestant, Moslem, Jew, Hindu, Buddhist—and within each faith there are practicing subdivisions. Every one of these ethnic and religious groups exists within a cultural setting dominated by secular values, education, and technology. The tension and contrast of fundamental values which define human identity are no longer a matter of passing interest. It is a matter of growing vital concern for every ethnic group that wants its identity to survive.

The clash of fundamental values at this level of frequency is new to human society and raises issues of coherence, applicability, and adequacy in the minds of the humans who feel it. Tourist travel, the immigration of large communities, and worldwide communication networks and media coverage have brought about this clash of values. It is increasingly difficult to live in an ethnic group that will not escape confrontation with other ways of being human. This is also true for religions and religious faiths.

I have concluded that if we humans seek to live with each other in peace, within a setting of any nation, the reality is that those who live in cities will experience sharp contrasts of ethnic values. We can no longer assume that one group is the majority and expect others to assimilate. Any one group is or soon will be a minority in relationship to all others. Tolerance implies that one has the power to grant acceptance but retains the power to withdraw the grant. I suggest we must move beyond tolerance to active acceptance of our differences. Acceptance of ethnic and religious differences must become the guiding value of our emerging secular global culture.

Over the last fifty years (1948-1998), I received my education, spent four years in the U.S. Navy, and served as a minister in 11 different cities in the U.S.A. During this time I lived for at least a year in 12 different states. This life style forced me to realize that some people are clearly citizens of a state, while others see themselves as citizens of the United States. Each state has its own defining pride and value set. Identification with the local sports teams is only one of the most obvious aspects of this value set. Moving so often has meant that I have had to enter and leave many communities or in-groups. There is a sense in which the United States is one country, but an underlying reality is that many citizens have strong loyalty to their home state and its concerns. Everyone of us participates in several **in-groups**, each defined by geography, an interest, our family, or work setting.

As a minister who has been trained to be conscious of values and how the people around me are using them, I entered into whatever community I was called into "this year" and made the value shifts from "last year" as needed. This series of moves gave me the opportunity (or did it pose a necessity?) to learn how to shift values in terms of the city, state, local climate, and "ethnic" milieu. As the years have gone along, a recurring sentence fragment, Life for the in-group with quality, emerged in my thinking that helped me describe, analyze, and when needed compare, the various value systems I was leaving and entering. And of course all this happened within an overlying pattern of culture, which we may call "American secular."

There are many ways to organize a consideration of values. This one has been very useful for me. It has come to form the basis for how I learn about any new community or group. There are two levels upon which values function: words and actions. In entering a new group or an established situation, keeping them separate was necessary for me to learn whether these two expressions of values were congruent or in tension with each other.

When I entered a new congregation, I read all the documents setting forth the identity and values, structure and process, of my new community. I listened to what people said were the events of their history, what they said was going on, and what they wanted to happen. Then I very carefully watched what was revealed in the actual events of living in community. Seldom did all of these levels of expressed values agree. The differences and tension points were neither good nor bad. They simply were the way things were. They revealed where hurts needed healing, issues of trust needed attention, ambiguity existed about the use of power, confusion reigned concerning the goals and morals that had and would shape this group, and who really was in the center of things and who was really not. The information so developed became the basis for my interim ministry with each congregation.

Life for the in-group with quality.... I developed this descriptive phrase as I moved within American culture, however, it is also applicable to history and to the continual political struggles and conflicts in our world. For instance, if we look at the Balkan states and the ongoing struggle for survival and control of land there, we can make sense of it only by separating what is said from what is done. Political and military action reveals the real operative values, no matter how speech is used to confuse. There are clear in-groups, and every person belongs to one or another. Fighting is supposed to decide which in-group will survive and with what quality, on what land, and with what religion.

To expand the meaning of the three key words in, life for the in-group with quality..., let me express each term as a double-edged commandment in Biblical form:

life means, Thou shalt survive and procreate;

in-group means, Thou shalt maintain self-respect and live in community;

quality means, Thou shalt think and use reverence.

It has taken me several years to understand the full richness and power of this value-clarifying statement. I have applied it to many situations, both present and historical. I have used it to help me understand what was going on in small groups, such as a family, and with large groups, such as a congregation or nation or religion. I find that as I understand how a given in-group gives meaning to each of the elements in words and deeds, two important systems of values are revealed. As the tensions between words and deeds become clear so does the crisis of integrity.

Within a group, formed by the collective sharing and interaction of many individuals, every individual has his or her place. A tension between the values of individuals and the values held by the group as a community is always present.

Newcomers have to sort out the values that define structure and others that govern process. My advice to other newcomers, from my experience with a dozen communities, is never neglect clarifying the values that have shaped the past from those values the members say they want to lead them into the future. In order to interact with a group realistically and effectively, one cannot neglect to note and account for who holds which values, who holds power to block or approve change, who wants change and will support it, who wants the values from the past to survive and control future events. Value analysis is not simple. It usually is very complex.

When I first formulated this value-clarification guideline, I thought of life as the primary and dominating value. Later I realized that individuals will give their lives for the survival of their in-group. Mothers will give their lives for their children. Youth will give their lives for their country. And in-groups will sacrifice much in a conflict over what quality of living will govern the future. Nations will go to war over the control of a piece of land or to save the world for democracy. After some years of reflection and observation, I believe that the three key words interact in surprising ways as determined by circumstance. How the elements of reverence are used determine which key word will govern in a situation and shift the balance between them. What perspectives and sense of proportion are used in a given situation?

I think that six ideas (survival, procreation, self-respect, community, thinking, and reverence) give meaning to these three key words (life, in-group, quality). Now let us briefly explore each idea:

1.   *In a sense, individual survival is primary.* However, individual survival has little value without procreation, making community essential for individual survival. It is also true that without community an individual's life is

reduced to the basics of getting food, water, shelter, and clothing.

Individually and collectively, human survival depends upon the health of the biosphere of our globe. This first commandment involves any individual in supporting values, which transcend the self as understood in individualism. Individual survival usually becomes identified with a community or in-group, and most individuals will give their lives for the benefit of other human beings. For most of us, this is a one-day-at-a-time process. I have given the last 30 years of my life in the service of my liberal religious tradition. Everyone gives his or her life to family or career or cause.

2. *Procreation has sex and birth of the next generation as its guiding reality and metaphor.* Human procreation is impossible without a community of two, plus many more to sustain a healthy gene pool. Procreation means passing on values to other people. Procreation for anyone may include passing on genes through conception and birth, passing on a way of life by teaching or raising children, perpetuating ideas through conversation and books, sustaining in-group identity through participation in the community, maintaining a religious faith through support of a religious community.

The commandment to procreate involves the individual in community or an in-group that is transcendent of the individual.

3. *Self-respect, in this model, comes from and is sustained by our interaction with other people.* Individual self-respect includes the mix, and sum total, of the passions or emotions, ideas, values, status, and senses of self-worth and place that sustains each person in their in-groups. Every in-group has boundaries that define its identity. In-groups have self-respect, and will react to perceived

insults to it. Self-respect has to do with sense of place, status, worth, dignity, the energy and effort a person or group is willing to expend in order to obtain or sustain a given condition of living. Self-respect sets boundaries and limits for us as persons and in-groups.

For any human being to know and use boundaries or limits involves an awareness of transcendence. To experience what is smaller requires a context of what is larger. Identifying what is different and, therefore, separated out on the other side of the limit or boundary is essential to developing self-respect.

4.   *Community begins with the community of cells that make up a person's body and becomes a broader area that includes groups of individuals who share commonly held values and work together to achieve them.* At the larger level every individual is a member of the human community and is a dependent participant within the community of living organisms here on Earth. This transcendent reality should never be forgotten or neglected at one level; at another, people are ultimately responsible for themselves.

The commandment to live in community is a transcendent paradox. The two values in this paradox are inseparable. Proportional balance between the elements of the paradox is essential to health of both individual and community, a fact often neglected by short-sighted human action plans.

5.   *Thinking includes how realistic human beings are* about their living conditions; how they use reason to accomplish and express their values; when and where they accept enough as enough; and how they use memory, imagination, and reflection to understand and survive in their world. Human emotions derive from our self-respect and are part of who we are.

The following questions will help discover a person's or group's way of thinking:

- Within their reality, how do they fulfill the requirements of adequacy and applicability to achieve immediate health and long term survival?
- What, if any, problems are there in the way they apply their spoken values in the material and spiritual world?
- What level of coherence does the living of the community have?
- Which values are applied with consistency and for whose benefit, and to whose detriment?

Even though these questions may prompt a productive level of specificity and clarity, this is obviously far from an exhaustive analysis of human thinking. The commandment, Thou shalt *think* (*that is*, be realistic and rational in response to world events) tells us that to achieve the quality we value in our living, we must use all these mental capacities to the fullest level of which we are capable. As a definition of function, not content, the quality of our living depends upon what and how we think and how we use our *sense of reverence* (*that is*, always being informed by a sense of perspective and proportion). This leaves the content of quality to be determined by each in-group and its historical circumstance.

6. *Thou shalt use reverence, tells us that the quality of our living depends upon how we, as individuals and in-groups, manage the relationships between ourselves and the larger group, the material and spiritual levels of our existence, competing values, and issues of trust, power, and goals.* Reverence is our capacity to sense and know transcendent perspective. We derive our values from these perspectives. In many situations needs and ideas of the good act as lures to action. The question to be resolved is, how will competing values be balanced and

given proportional weight to insure the health and
vitality of the group and the individuals who are its
members?

The first task of reverence is to enable individuals or groups of
individuals to define how they will live as an in-group with acceptable
quality. Reverence suggests we must consider various perspectives,
balancing the competing values proportionally in healthy and successful
ways. No solution to this problem will be all good. Some good will be
sacrificed to realize the good chosen. Reason tends to select one value and
pursue it to perfection. I believe reason is not adequate to the task of
achieving unadulterated good; in our capitalistic society's selection of
wealth as a good, for example, its pursuit by reason results in greed which
threatens to destroy our world with pollution. Wealth is a good; having it,
feels good. However, if you do not know what to do with it after
becoming wealthy, it becomes meaningless. Many Americans have much
wealth and are using it only for personal pleasure. Too few are using it for
the good of our human community or for the long-term health of our
planet Earth.

Reverence tells us to value every particular thing within the perspective
of the transcending whole of which it and we are apart. Using reverence
seeks to insure that we will act with an appropriate sense of proportion in
our value system so that short-term goods lead to transcendent health and
vitality for self and community. Reverence keeps the means we choose to
achieve our ends consistent with those ends. It is by using reverence that
anyone may balance the competing demands of the six commandments
derived from the sentence fragment, life for the in-group with quality...

I believe reverence is much neglected in secular society. Reverence
needs to be given as much attention as reason, if we human beings are to
use science and technology for the benefit and health of all living
organisms. Maintaining or improving the health of our Earth as an

organic biochemical and geophysical entity needs our balanced use of reverence and reason.

Moral Values

Now let me move on to a few ideas about morality. It seems to me that our world has room for many moral codes. Every tribe, nation, religious group, or people has its own. The essence of each set of moral values is consistent application expected by the person or community upholding it. Moral codes of values have specific content derived from religion or the identity of a people or tradition for which it is operable. Every set derives its power from the authority from which it is said to come and gains authority from the consequences an in-group imposes on violators. All sets of moral values have the expectation of *consistent* application within and for the in-group.

"Life for the in-group with quality," may be used to help describe what morality an individual or group is using or to prescribe what morality should be. To use this phrase descriptively, observation is needed to identify what values are expressed in the words and actions of individuals in a group. Observation gives the content to each the three key words in it. To use the sentence prescriptively involves decision, imposition, and authority. Someone decides that a particular content is better or preferred over another and then sets about imposing it on other human beings. Religious missionaries and law enforcement are examples of this.

Perhaps one of the most common reasons for concluding that a given morality is better than another is the judgment or opinion that one is more inclusive than the other. For example, the morality that seeks to keep a person or party in political office in the name of national security is less inclusive than the morality of the U.S. Constitution, which applies the rule of law to all Americans. When a group of people commits ethnic cleansing for revenge or to insure the survival of their in-group, they are judged guilty of crimes against humanity. This judgment makes use of a more inclusive or transcendent morality over a set of values held by a smaller group of people.

Most people I know want their set of moral values to be considered absolute. They want theirs to be applied without exception and with precedence over all others. Particularly, this is so if the result benefits them. If a religion completely dominates a people, its set of morals may be applied with absolute authority. However, in our world of many in-groups, each with a set of moral values, not one of them is absolute. All moral values are relative to the in-group that lives by them.

If two or more sets of moral values are compared to each other, one or the other may be judged more inclusive or more universal in application. This implies that one is transcendent of the other. However, the two sets of values may be just different. For example, a set of values that applies to only one race or ethnic group is transcended by a set of morals that applies to all human beings. All the identified groups in the Balkans are seeking to survive. They are killing each other. The larger human community is judging the results of their fighting by a transcendent set of values that concludes that crimes against humanity have been committed.

Relevant to sets of moral values, there are two expectations for consistency:

1.   They will apply to all members of the in-group, and
2.   All members of the in-group will apply them consistently over time.

An implication is that moral values do not necessarily apply to individuals who are not members of the in-group. Second, recognized membership in an in-group is important for survival. Third, there are many in-groups between every individual and humanity. The larger or more inclusive or more transcendent the in-group, the greater force their morality is usually accorded in human judgment.

"Do unto others as you would have them do unto you," is a content statement for giving consistent value to self and others. To say it comes from God gives it transcendent authority. To say it applies to all people of whatever in-group gives it universal application. While this idea of morality is fundamental for many in-groups, Jesus stretched its meaning by teaching that "others" include family, friends, companions, and enemies.

American history illustrates that in-group status is important for survival and quality of life. Just whom the Constitution grants protection to and whom the law protects evolved over time. Our struggle in the civil rights movement has been about who will be included in the in-group and to whom morality applies. The recognition that consistency is the essence of morality is to ground morals in our human capacity for reasoning. This suggests that morals are relative to in-groups and contribute to the quality each seeks to make real. Every in-group has a set of morals, a set of values, which define its identity, and makes membership an advantage for individuals.

Any set of moral values may be judged for internal consistency and coherence. Is it consistently applied to all individuals who are said to be members of the in-group? Are all Americans given equal protection by the police and equal treatment by the justice system? Clearly, morals are a set of values described in mere words, and what actually happens in the physical and social world may be very different from the ideal called for in the moral code. Whether, or to what extent, the members of an in-group actually live their lives according to the dictates of their moral values is a judgment of consistent application. Under what circumstances will a moral code be strictly enforced? Does loyalty in peace and war mean the same thing? Does treason to an in-group's well-being carry the same consequences in peace and war?

Another way to compare moral codes of values is to look at their limits of application. Does this set of moral values sustain life and the quality of living over time, over hundreds of years? Does it work effectively for different peoples and differing cultures? Over how many differing times and ethnic in-groups will it work to bring vitality, vibrance, and peace to all? To whom is it expected to apply? And to whom does it not apply? This functional understanding of morals separates the content of the values to be applied from the source which an in-group claims to have drawn them. In human history, sets of morals gained power to control members of an in-group because they were said to come from God, the state, a King, covenant, constitution, dictator, family, clan, corporation, and nation.

Let me consider one other important way that values function in our living. This is our human capacity for sin. As I wrote in Chapter 6, to sin means to miss the intended mark, to miss the good in life. In a functional understanding of values, one cannot proceed without accepting that human beings do see the good in life, act to achieve it, and miss the mark with great frequency.

We human beings identify the good and pursue it with great consistency. I suggest that every human always acts for the good. The results are not always what is expected. In fact, in my life, the results of my actions for the good are seldom exactly what I intended. Many times we must choose between two equally undesirable options. However, when we choose and act, we are acting for the least undesirable of the two and, therefore, the good. We use our reason and reverence to aid us in the pursuit of the good. We imagine what the good, perfectly realized, would be and adopt this as our goal. When we pursue perfection with consistency, we tend to go too far. We turn the good into something else. The dream of perfection frequently lures us to sin. We know food is essential to living, but eat too much. We learn money will buy security and comfort, but then become dominated by greed.

Let me illustrate how sin works in our living with a story from A.A. Milne's *Winnie the Pooh* in which Pooh is wandering through the forest one day and hears a buzzing. He sits down to think (reason), and his logic goes this way: "I hear a buzzing, buzzing means bees, bees mean honey, and honey means something for me to eat." This is good reasoning, if only a little colored by the sin of self-centeredness (illustration I).

Then Pooh bear does what you and I would do. He goes after the honey by the most direct means available. He climbs the tree from which the buzzing is coming, getting impatient and distracted just as most humans would. He sings a song to himself, and then reaches for the honey just before it is within reach. He overreaches himself and falls through the branches to land in a prickle bush. We frequently overreach the reality of who we are (sin illustration II).

Pooh still wants the bee's honey and so he goes to Christopher Robin's house to enlist him in deceiving the bees. Pooh selects a blue balloon and rolls in the mud so as to look like a little black cloud up in the blue sky. After the balloon is blown up, Pooh floats up even with the bees' nest and 20 feet out from it with no breeze to blow him nearer. To increase the deception Christopher Robin walks up and down with an opened umbrella and says, "Tut, tut, it looks like rain." The bees get suspicious, as Pooh finds out when one inflicts pain to his nose. (sin illustration III is complete.) A deception is a denial of reality, a lie. This case is funny to us, but Pooh pays the price by being stung.

So Christopher Robin aims his gun ever so carefully and fires. "OW!" says Pooh. "Did I miss?" asks Christopher Robin. "No, but you missed the balloon," says Pooh. So Christopher Robin fires again and Pooh comes gently to the ground. The final sin in this story is an historical allusion. Christopher aims with a weapon and misses, even though he aimed so very carefully and with full intent to hit the target, which was not Pooh. Please note that this wonderful story, freighted with meaning about human living, also reveals to us that we will pay a price in the here and now when we sin. Pooh falls out of the tree into a gorse bush, gets stung by a bee, receives an "Owie" when Christopher Robin misses the balloon. Then Pooh's arms are stuck sticking up in the air for a week after holding on to the balloon for so long in his sinful attempt to get the bees' honey.

If we human beings pursue our goals exclusively from within our reason we will never know when it is enough. We will go too far every time. We will find sin our constant companion. It is reverence, a sense of transcendent perspective and proportion, that informs us of when enough is enough. With a greater use of reverence, we may avoid sin and be much more fulfilled as spiritually healthy human beings.

My point is that use of reason brings both good news and bad news. It gives us morality, on the one hand, and also is a major element that drives us to sin. Using human reason in both cases needs to be done within a context of the transcending reality within which life takes place. Reverence needs to inform our use of reason by keeping our actions in transcendent perspective and in proportion for health and goodness.

Chapter 11.

Christology

The basic definition of **religion**, which we are using, is what individuals and communities do with the solitariness of individual human beings. Religion is how individuals deepen and enrich their understanding and acceptance of their involvement in communities that transcend the individual and learn to live with constant change that we know as the creativity of our Universe. This is a functional definition of religion and is not dependent upon any given religious tradition for its meaning. I believe that all established religious traditions fulfill this function. They bring meaning, spiritual health, and vitality into human living by enabling individuals to accept and thrive within the transcending systems of reference within which our human living is embedded and dependent.

Christianity meets all these goals for its followers. So does Judaism, Islam, and Hinduism. Each is a powerful example of how religion responds to human solitariness with a web of meaning reaching out to the transcendent systems of reference surrounding every individual. Over the last several centuries Christian meanings have dominated the English-speaking world and, therefore, theological words are defined in the content of Christianity. Christology is usually known as the study of God becoming a human in Jesus, the stories about him, what they reveal about our living, and the way all this is celebrated in symbols.

In the last 50 years secular culture has grown to be a significant influence in western culture. I think it is not too much of a stretch to observe that secular ideas and technology have become equal to, if not more influential than, Christianity in our modern culture. Add to this the patterns of migration of peoples of all the world religions so that every country and city of any size has noticeable communities of immigrants living there who call the place home. One can no longer act as if Christianity is the only religion.

Therefore, I suggest we need to recognize that the word Christ is a Greek word meaning one who is anointed to be the savior, and ask, "What does each religion do to save the people who find the meaning of their lives by following its traditions?" I answer that they use symbols to dramatize meaning drawn from their transcendent reference systems as the basis for living with faith and hope, understanding and acceptance, love and purpose. **Christology**, as I define it, is the study of how religions use symbols. The way Christianity uses Jesus, as a symbol, is an example of this activity. Jesus is only the central symbol used by Christianity. The Torah is the unifying symbol of Judaism, as I understand it.

The purpose of religion in the lives of individuals is to know and celebrate a web of meaning that responds to the questions or anxiety raised by the individuals knowing solitariness. Every web of meaning is made up of relationships between each individual and the elements of the surrounding systems of transcending reference. These connections are real but not necessarily obvious. They are all around us, yet we may walk by them in ignorance. It is like the walls of the house someone has lived in for 25 years. Over the years the walls have gotten very dirty, but this may go unnoticed. So religion's task is to symbolize and dramatize the relationships that give meaning to human living. Religion's task is to involve human beings in concrete activities, which are understood to be symbolic of more abstract relationships.

Rituals and Symbols

A **ritual** is an action that is repeated and understood to be real in and of itself. It is intended to remind us through its symbolic aspect of one or more layers of meaning and connection. The repetition is important because only as we experience the ritual enough so that it becomes well known, and well known under numerous situations, will it gain richness and power of meaning. We humans learn rituals usually under relatively casual circumstances. The ritual may lack power until we use it under stress or as a response to trauma. A ritual's full symbolic power and meaning will only be known as one participates in it as a response to a real experience and feels how the symbolic connections do make sense.

If a ritual is to have real power in our lives, there has to come a moment after we have been doing it when we have a flash of insight and connection. We feel and know, "Oh, so this is what I have been doing and why!" In the church of my boyhood the minister always wore a robe, although many Unitarian ministers did not. When I started preaching, I tried not wearing a robe, but one Sunday I realized I was not honoring fully the tradition that had shaped me. I was treating conducting worship as if it were something not very special in the life to that congregation. Without the robe, I was unable to step from ordinary living into the role of minister/preacher. "Oh, I see," I said to myself, "if this sacred tradition is to be fully honored, I need some psychic space to step into the pulpit!"

Years later I began serving a congregation the members of which had a history of objecting to their minister wearing a robe. It was too powerful a symbol of the scars left by the religious experiences of their youth. If I was to minister to them, I could not wear a robe. I had to be with them in this way if I was to minister to them in so many other ways. I still needed a ritual to remind me of what I was doing as I led worship, so I dedicated a three-piece suit for leading Sunday worship in that congregation. I wore it every Sunday and only on Sunday or for memorial and wedding services, never for other occasions.

Worship during the practice of a religion may be the most obvious time and place in which symbols are used. I suggest that a functional definition of worship is a symbolic drama of an event or relationship and its meaning for human living within the transcendent context that surrounds individual solitariness. For example, every Christian funeral retells the Jesus story, gives the Christian interpretation that faith in Jesus as the Christ brings life after death, and seeks to use this particular grief experience to renew and intensify faith in Jesus as a response to individual solitariness.

When a wedding is intended to be a worship service, it is a symbolic drama of a man and woman committing themselves in marriage, giving this event and relationship meaning within a particular religious tradition. Usually a man and woman are lifting their relationship as friends, companions, and lovers to that of husband and wife or partners in union. This shift usually has significance for an extended family. And they are asked to be present to acknowledge and bless the new quality of the relationship.

Every religion I know of has prescribed or suggested rituals for responding to the death of a companion or loved one. The purpose of a funeral or memorial service is to put a period at the end of one life and to affirm the faith of the living who are attending and grieving. Every funeral uses the symbols of the faith chosen for the service with trust and hope that the life ended was of worth and that every life is of worth, even as one knows with new certainty that life ends in death.

Symbols are things, entities, and activities that we understand to have multiple layers of meaning. A symbol is an object or activity that is used in the concrete present and intended to be the basis for a metaphor. Religious symbols remind us of or draw our attention to relationships that are not obvious, and yet are important to the religious meaning of our living.

Traditionally, space set aside for worship has been designed with a celebration of the transcendent included in the architecture. The transcendent is symbolized by the vertical in Christianity, a circle in Earth-centered religions, and a mandala in both Buddhism and Hinduism. The space becomes a place where the horizontal, as a symbol of the plane on which we live, and the transcendent intersect. In contrast, humanist congregations of the 1960s built meeting rooms that are multi-purpose boxes. There was no celebration of the vertical because they were seeking to down play the transcendent. They said they found the meaning of living from within the human community. Many such meeting rooms for worship also had no windows thereby shutting out sunlight and a view of nature. The symbolism is that the focus should be on only the human community. Some would say the choice of design was purely economics, but one could also surmise a lack of awareness of architecture as a powerful symbol expressing the purpose of religious community. Many humanists say they find the transcendent in nature, but it is strange that in so many humanist worship areas nature is shut out. There are no windows.

It is interesting to observe how light is used in buildings intended for religious purposes. Some religious traditions hold that religious faith and activity in our living is a source of light and hope. There are lots of windows to let the world and sun light in. Others present the church as a sanctuary from the world, which is in some way threatening: buildings are of stone, windows are small or made of stained glass, the sanctuary feels dark and is meant to be a place of safety. To know the meaning of light as a symbol, ask how light is used. Its interpretation reveals the religious faith of the congregation. More may be said about financial history than religious meaning in the building a congregation is using. However, by paying attention to the use of both height and light, you can easily tell something powerful about the faith of the congregation. If the members know that using symbols is one of the central functions of their religious community, they will pay attention.

Where furniture is placed in a room used for worship may be symbolic. In many traditional sanctuaries, the pulpit is built-in, usually higher that the congregation's seating, and symbolizes that the words coming from it come from a transcendent source—the use of the vertical, again. In one church I served the pulpit was big and heavy and had always been center stage, although it could be set off center with a little effort. The organ was in the center of the balcony, although the balcony was big enough to put the console somewhere else. These examples illustrate that the spoken word and the use of music in the tradition of that church were central to the worship service. At Christmas time I moved the pulpit off center by just a few feet and used the stage for an arrangement of greens, candles, and flowers. I was saying with symbols that aesthetics in this season are as important as shared rational words. I was reminding the members that even the rational words have a symbolic level, which points beyond to transcendent meaning.

Today many rooms used for worship use movable stacking chairs to give flexibility. One should be conscious of group dynamics in arranging the chairs. Many seem to rush to put the chairs in circles, wanting to symbolize that gathering for worship in a safe place is where we share common values. I think this is appropriate for services that are intended to be a joyous celebration of a good in living. However, I use circles with great care. I believe that religion is what individual do with their solitariness. If there is laughter or tears during the church service, something really happened to someone who was drawn out of rational control. The service touched them at an emotional or a spiritual level. What was said or done connected something important to them.

If the chairs are in rows or slightly curving rows, each person sitting in them has a degree of personal space in which his or her public mask of control may be dropped. Rows give each person a small place for a degree of privacy, while still being among all the other people in the room. When chairs are in circles, everyone is facing a lot of people; everyone is on stage. This is an environment with little sense of honoring individual solitariness within the community. Circles of chairs during worship presume that the community is safe for all participants which everyone may not know or feel.

The movements of the people participating in the service are the dance of the service. Even the choice of where to stand may be symbolic. A priest usually stands in the chancel to give the benediction, using the raised altar space as a symbol that the blessing comes through him from God. The vertical is used again as the symbol of the ultimate transcendent.

Unitarian Universalist congregations honor **congregational polity**. This means that the power in the church comes from and is vested in the congregation as opposed to the clergy, tradition, institution, creeds, or a book. When I give the benediction I stand as a member of the congregation. I am consciously symbolizing that in our tradition religious truth and blessings come through the congregation, and I speak for the transcendent power they represent as I say the benediction. So reflect with care about the symbolic value of simple bodily placement for activities during a worship service.

Words are symbols also, of course. Many traditional Christian ministers say at the conclusion of weddings, "I pronounce you husband and wife." For years I have said instead, "I announce, and we all recognize, that you are husband and wife." In our liberal religious tradition, I believe that the couple marries each other. They create a bond which I as a minister may bless and the state may sanction, but the couple creates it and together they must sustain it. Using the word "pronounce," implies that the couple is not married until the priest or clergy says they are. In contrast, my announcement emphasizes that the responsibility for sustaining the marriage rests with the new partnership.

Many worship services include singing by choir and congregation because the reality of group singing is that it creates a powerful experience of community and togetherness for those doing it. Every individual stands with everyone else, and everyone sings the same words. This kind of musical expression touches the emotional side of our beings. When people sing together, they even have to breathe together. Singing is a powerful symbol and experience of community. Participants cooperate and share during this activity at a profound level.

I have used examples from my own ministry to illustrate how important symbols are to religious activity. I do not intend to push any one religion or a single religious content. I mean to suggest that the simplest elements of our living may have symbolic meaning. The shape and form of a building, the use of light and colors, where one stands and how one moves, what one says and how one says it, how chairs are arranged—all these elements may be used as symbols to draw our attention to the ways individuals are related to *the transcendent reference systems of meaning.*

Symbols and Community Life

When entering a new religious community before my retirement, I asked the following questions:

- What are these individuals doing with their solitariness?
- What transcendent reference systems of meaning are they concerned with?
- How do they symbolize the relationships between each individual and the transcendent reference systems?
- What traditions have they honored in the past three years and what do they expect this year?
- What rituals and symbols are expected, and what symbols will be missed if they are not used?
- What unique ways of using symbols does this congregation have?
- How open are they to some changes in style or substance?
- What things and activities do they recognize as symbolic?
- What things are functioning as symbols of meaning that they do not recognize as having this level of significance?

This last question was frequently the most important one. It let me find out what issues concerning trust, boundaries, faith, and group identity were present and might need attention. For instance, a non-event could carry symbolic meaning.

In one congregation I served, only one person knew all the detailed financial information. Although I was told this was so because others were not interested, I understood it to be a mask for problems of trust. The Board of Trustees did not have enough information to act independently of this one individual, so he had great power—too much power. Money matters frequently reveal the level of trust in the congregation and the level of honesty within the group process. I moved to get monthly reports to the Board of Trustees printed and a summary of the financial information made available to all members on request. Trust grew, and giving to the community also increased. The absence of financial information within the public realm was a symbol of a trust problem that had many other symptoms when I went looking for them.

In another congregation I noted that the Bylaws included nothing about the relationship and mutual responsibilities of the Board to and with the staff to the congregation. This absence suggested that there could be issues about trust. An oral tradition, in which everyone knew what each needed to know or they could ask someone who did, was deemed sufficient. Of course, only a few knew who really knew what one needed to know. I asked how anyone new to the group could trust it when there were so many rules that seemed secret and which could only be learned by breaking one and suffering embarrassment?

Christology is the study of how symbols are used as a vital part of any religion. This functional definition of a word usually limited to one religion may help achieve understanding among the world's major religions. Let me conclude by suggesting that every religion's symbols should:

1. *Create a web of transcendent meaning* dramatized in ways that sustain the spiritual health of individuals as they respond to their solitariness.

2. *Shape a web of meaning that is realistic, adequate, and applicable* to the human condition and to the cultures of individuals and communities involved.

3.   *Dramatize faith and hope by symbols that are relevant* to the people they serve. This means they must be coherent and applicable with all aspect of their lives and consistent with their understanding of themselves.

4.   *Remind us of our human needs for reverence,* specifically our need for a transcendent perspective of ourselves and the present, and our need for a sense of proportion as we balance value priorities. It is from this sense of balance that we humans know when, "It is enough!" Our capacity for faith, thanksgiving, forgiveness, mercy, compassion, love, grief, hope, loyalty, trust, humor all depend upon our use of reverence.

5.   *Use ordinary things and activities as symbols.* Without their use, religion cannot fulfill its function in meeting our religious needs.

Chapter 12

Epistemology

The purpose of this chapter is not to tell all religions what they should know. However, it does set forth some of the problems they must deal with in their own traditions, if they are to be successful in our world's emerging secular culture.

Epistemology is usually a philosophical discipline concerning questions of how humans know anything. In this essay it means how we gain religious knowledge. Normally it has not been of much concern to theology. Theology assumes that through living in a religious community, listening to preaching, attending worship services, growing up with religious education which imparts tradition and dogma, and participating in study groups, one will come to know God or a specific religious tradition. One will come to know and accept a personal identity, which includes a particular way of being religious.

I believe these have been the assumptions of most Christian congregations in America. They were valid until the last 40 years or so. When Christianity dominated our culture and met no serious challenge or option prior to this time, acting as if Christianity were the only source of religious values made sense. As secular culture has gained in power and influence in human living, many followers of Christianity feel defensive. Christianity is not alone in its defensiveness. Any religion in a culture with a growing swell of secular values can no longer act as if it is the only source of people's knowledge. Secular values are another source. All religions must learn to survive and prosper within the context of secular culture.

Roman Catholicism has felt the threat of outside influences in the lives of its followers for several generations. With the leadership of its priests, American Catholics founded the system of schools to ensure that the Roman Catholic perspective of life was included in daily course work. It is interesting to note that the Catholic Church seems to be having staffing and financial problems maintaining their separate school system, as secular culture gains strength in America. Today other Christian groups are starting their own schools to ensure that non-Catholic, but still Christian, religious ideas are part of their children's education.

Maintaining the identity and integrity of being a Jew has always been a struggle for Jews. They have a history of being a minority in an overwhelming culture, which has at times accepted them, at times tolerated them, and at times persecuted them. Jews take very seriously the challenge of how their children will come to know and stay identified with the Jewish community. Many religious groups are now facing this same problem in a way they have not before.

The rise of fundamentalist movements in many of the established world religions seem to me to be a reaction against the rising tide of secular influence around our world. The conditions of living are changing in most countries. The expectations of material comfort are rising in many locations. The understanding of what it means to be human is changing also. The established rules drawn in many cases from religion or ethnic traditions are being challenged. Dress codes for women are one example of this. How people dress is a symbol of status and role within the family and society. Fundamentalists resist these changes by asserting the power and goodness of the old ways. Yet secular materialism offers better health, more comfort in living, and with these changes come new images of human identity.

All of these events are examples of what we know about being human and living in community with each other, and how we come to know these things.

Epistemology must become a major and conscious concern for all religions. No, let me say it another way. How we human beings know and what we know about ourselves and the realms that transcend us must become a major concern of secular society, as well as of those who are concerned with religious matters. How human beings come to know anything and, in this case particularly, to know the things a religion considers important needs to become a major concern if it has not become so already. I believe this to be so because the health of individuals and communities depends upon how we human beings use our capacities for reasoning, reverence, and being realistic. Do we balance and integrate all three of these ways of responding to living? Only as we achieve a balanced use of all three will our living be healthy, vital, and vibrant.

Especially is this true for Christianity because it has been the dominant influence on our European-American culture over the last several hundred years. Now there is a new influence that is growing in strength. If secular culture is not already dominant in Europe and America, it soon will be. Through the spread of democratic, capitalistic ideas and ways of doing things, secular culture is invading every nation and country. So-called *scientific technology* is a third element contributing to secular culture. The emerging world economy and system of international affairs is creating a single global culture, which is based on secular technology. Telecommunications and the Internet are binding all people together in ways that were not possible 25 years ago.

It seems to me that the growing dominance of secular culture is an obvious reality of our world. What is not so obvious is that this process is strongly influencing what human beings know and how they know it. First, there are the facts and skills needed to function in the secular society: how one uses running water, flushes a toilet, uses electricity for light, and gets things done. To mention a few more examples, consider how one drives a car and follows traffic rules, flies on an airplane, deals with newspapers, magazines, and TV, or uses a computer.

After facts and skills come metaphors of understanding that shape who we are and who we understand ourselves to be. So many mechanical gadgets surround us that the metaphor of a mechanical world and mechanical self is one way to make sense of what it means to be human. However, if you are computer literate and sensitive to the more complicated ways an electro-mechanical machine works, a different metaphor suggests itself. These metaphors suggest that if a part of a human being breaks or malfunctions, the solution is to replace the part. Someone is always in control of a machine. They turn it on and off, and control its speed of operating. Mechanical metaphors suggest that our world works like a machine and we are the operators. We should be in control, even if we are not. With a little more study and some more knowledge, we will be able to predict and, therefore, control the elements of our world and ourselves.

We clearly have power over all the appliances and wonderful gadgets in our homes and offices. At least we do as long as the electric grid supplies us with power, the gas pipelines supply fuel, and the sewer system carries away our waste. This power-over situation is so pervasive, it suggests a metaphor or attitude to govern our relationship with the whole world. It suggests that our relationship to reality should be the same—*power over*. This is a metaphoric leap, an invalid one. We are dependent on all gadgets, and trust them to make living easier. We are dependent on the transcendent reality in which we live to be consistent and supportive of us. We need to include trust and dependence as major elements, as we understand and interact with our world and the reality that sustains us.

Some people like machines so much that they say human beings are like machines. But we are organisms, not machines, and therefore an organic metaphor is more appropriate to make sense of human living. When a bone is broken in a living organism, it is a very different matter than a tire going flat on a bike. You have to allow the bone to heal. Going to the store, buying a new bone, and installing it will not work. In contrast, I own and use my lawn mower and computer, but I live with my wife and family. *Living with* is not controlling. Honoring my wife's integrity and her as a person is very different from caring for our cars and the heating system of our house. Conception, pregnancy, and birth are how a baby comes to be. This is very different from setting up a wood shop and buying lumber to make a bookcase.

The metaphors we use to understand who we are and how we participate in the world that transcends us dictate what we do and how we interact with those things and people around us. Metaphors that shape our thinking determine our values and perspective of our place in the *transcendent reference systems* supporting and surrounding us. The question I am raising is how these and other metaphors drawn from secular ways of knowing influence what each individual does with their experience of solitariness.

Because I have tried to establish a new way to converse about religion, I may make some people uncomfortable in now presenting some contrasts. My point in this effort is to clarify trends or tendencies, which I understand to be actual dimensions of our culture. I will accentuate the tensions and differences between religion and secular culture. I expect that some people will not have experienced or seen some of these contrasts with the sharpness words give them.

Remember what I mean by religion. I accept that religion in the future will be a part of secular culture. The function of every religion is to enable individuals and communities of individuals to respond to the fact of human solitariness. To do this, religions must enable those they serve to deepen and integrate their relatedness within the *transcendent systems of reference* of self, community, and the creativity of our Universe. Individuals are religious as they fulfill this function in their living. How may religions ensure that their concerns are known, accepted, and honored in secular culture? Since this is a question of knowing, it is an epistemological question.

Epistemological Problems

All traditions must consider these emerging problems:

1.   *How will our human sense of transcendence be sustained in a culture which honors counting beans* and short-term measurable benefit? As the power and success of materialism increases with ever-newer technology, how will our human need for a sense of transcendent perspective and proportion be maintained? Who will teach it? How will it be taught?

2.   *Individualism has become a strong guiding set of values in the United States* in recent years. How will we balance this trend with every person's need for and dependence on community? Individualism posits that every person is independent, yet every one of us is dependent and cannot live unless we are involved in trusting other human beings and the natural world that supports us. How will the values of community be learned in a secular world that accentuates individualism so strongly?

3.   *In a world that rewards doing things and the more the better, how will the need for and value of being be sustained?* In secular culture one gets paid for what one does. Religion accepts that doing is important and also says that to be alive is good. Taking time to reflect, to appreciate, to *just be* is also important. As one ages, self-worth grounded in *being* becomes of ever-greater importance. As the number of people over age 65 increases, our society will need to give greater honor to being. Self-worth grounded in being derives its power from knowledge of the self within a transcendent perspective of space, time, and living. If we are always

busy doing, doing, doing, we will never have time to
know and explore that which is transcendent of the
present moment, the current activity, our focused
concern in the now. If older individuals can not let go of
doing and accept the value of being, they will experience
little comfort and joy in years past 65.

4.   *Secular culture has a tendency to value the short term* over
the longer term, profits this quarter over long-range
investment, the result this day over the outcome after
five years. People living and guided by secular values tend
to get the job done, sacrificing the quality that will take
more time to accomplish. In contrast, values drawn from
a religious perspective ask us to always include in our
valuing the transcendent: the longer time frame, the
communities of others and all living organisms, the
larger context within which we are living and acting.
How will we balance the tension between short-term
goals and the values that derive from considering a
transcendent perspective?

5.   What will become of grace? Two dimensions of reality
are *cause-and-effect,* which we may learn to predict and
control, and *grace,* the exquisite timing of events that
permeates our living and is ever present with us. We do
not control grace and never will, nor should we expect
to. Whether this is due to the complexity of the ultimate
transcendence of our universe or just to the nature of
reality, I do not know. It is something I have come to
accept. We may anticipate events flowing from grace, but
that is very different from controlling them.

Many situations in life are beyond our control. We are dependent upon
too many factors. In these situations we may do things that will almost
ensure the result we desire will not happen, or we may do things that will
make the desired result much more likely to occur. Both cause-and-effect
and grace are revealed to those who have the eyes to see, the ears to hear,
and the mind and heart to understand. With secular education
emphasizing how cause-and-effect works, what source of education about
grace will we include in our society?

6. *How will we human beings resolve the tension between the
    twin realities, control and helplessness?* We are to some
    extent in control of our living and to some extent
    helpless, as we face the events of each day. If control is
    the guiding value in our living, how will we learn to trust
    and live comfortably with being dependent? Resolving
    this tension is one of the major spiritual issues upon
    which the health of this generation and future
    generations depends.

7. *How will individuals come to accept that they are aging and
    biologically slowing down, but still sustain a sense of self-
    worth?* Secular culture places a high value on doing and
    youthful vitality. How will death and dying be accepted
    and faced in a culture that ignores and discounts
    transcendent perspective? In secular culture there needs
    to be an active tension between facts and meaning.

8. *The dilemma of facts versus meaning.* Secular culture tends
    to like facts. Religion depends on and strives to deliver
    meaning. If religions fade into disuse, what source of
    meaning and purpose in living will there be? Meaning
    comes to human beings as they experience and interpret
    the transcendent reference systems of relatedness

surrounding them. So I ask again, today and in our
future, what sources of knowing transcendent perspective
and proportion are active and will be honored as vital to
human health? What institution is teaching reverence as
equally important as reasoning? Where does one go
today to learn how to balance and integrate the power of
both reason and reverence within a realistic
understanding of life and living?

One of the conclusions of this functional understanding of religion is
that values held and acted upon by an individual come from and are
dependent upon the *transcendent systems of reference and meaning* that the
individual knows and accepts. Most individuals in the past have gained
experience and knowledge of these connections from the communities
they live within. What source of this connection will there be in our
culture as it is shaped more and more by the ideas derived from secular
society? Values are derived from the meaning people hold, not from facts
they know. In these contrasts, secular culture values facts over meaning
and religion values meaning over facts. Yes, both sides need both; however,
each has a preference. I am arguing for equal value to be given to both.

9.   *Secular materialism values rewards given*, pay earned,
       status and prestige recognized, wealth accumulated. I
       suggest that the knowledge of enough comes from
       another source—religion and reverence. From the secular
       side of our society, I feel pressure for gaining more and
       more until greed is the driving force in a person's living.
       It is from religion that I hear values derived from letting
       go and acting upon, "It is enough."

Spiritual Health through Reverence

As I observe secular society, I see the glorification of the individual.
Individual independence and dignity are stressed. Power to and for the

individual is frequently valued at the expense of the community. Individuals seek power and ever more power. This has a tendency to become *power over* that has a tendency to lose sight of justice and seek revenge. When mistakes are made or a wrong is done, punishment and revenge tend to be the response. I submit that forgiveness would lead to greater health for the individual and community in many situations. However, our society will not give full and appropriate honor to forgiveness until we acknowledge and develop our capacity for reverence to a level equal to that which we accord reason. The act of forgiving depends on a transcendent perspective that places short-term insult and anger in a longer and larger context of personal and community health and peace.

Underlying all of these tensions is the idea that knowing transcendence is important for human spiritual health. And physical and spiritual health are mutually dependent. **Spiritual health** is the degree to which an individual has come to know, integrate, and use reverence. Reverence is our human capacity to sense transcendence, shift the transcendent perspective we view the world with, and give proportional balance to the values flowing from these different perspectives. The survival of every functioning, healthy, vital human culture requires an adequate and creative use of reverence. Knowing how to use reverence depends upon understanding transcendence.

I think there are four dimensions through which we humans come to know transcendence. All are important. Each teaches something different. As all four work together a richness emerges that is lost if one of them is not involved. They are time, place, experience, and the use of language.

- *Time* we know and deal with through memory and imagination. The past and future transcend the present; as we remember and what we remember enriches our experience of the present. Memories give us our identity, values, and sense of worth. Shared religious history of "my" people binds people together. As we use imagination we are able to plan, dream, have fantasies, know the value of present activity. Meaningful action in the present is dependent upon realistic imagining of the future, and creativity is dependent upon an active imagination. Experiencing time passing is a way of knowing change. Our knowledge of contrast comes from our experience of change and noted differences. Without experiencing contrast and knowing the significance of it, we would not develop our capacity for reverence.

I have just retired after 31 years of ministry and six years of moving every year. During those last years I remembered all the people I had worked with and all the cities I had passed through. Gradually I gained an insight and longed to stay put. The tension between the values I served as interim minister gradually became secondary to my need to be in one place, have a home, and spend enough time to enjoy a few deep friendships. It was the memories of times past that gave me a transcendent perspective of the present and allowed me to let go of all the values I had served for so many years.

- By *place* I point to how each individual fits into family, city, work, nation, humanity, nature, Universe. What sense of physical location does every individual have and need? How do we human beings come to know each of these? What relevance do they have for us? How does knowing about them influence our appreciation of size, vastness, smallness, security? How do these surrounding reference systems of transcendence shape one's sense of mystery, self, belonging? How does each individual understand these transcendent contexts? As one's experience and understanding of these different levels of transcendence grow and deepen, one's sense of self and

what it means to be human changes. Everyone's sense of
self is dependent upon how these levels of transcendence
are integrated.

People who have lived on a family farm all their lives have a strong
sense of connection and ownership of the land. Who they are is tied to
those acres of trees and fields. A person living in a city is familiar with how
the streets are laid out, where buildings and houses are and what they look
like, how green areas flow and mingle with everything else. City people
will accept small changes without much fuss, however, big ones will call
forth resistance. These feelings illustrate how the place we live is
embedded in a transcendent context. This context is crucial to who we
understand ourselves to be.

When NASA obtained and published those beautiful pictures of our
world taken from the moon, we were given a transcendent perspective of
where we are and who we are in the larger vastness of the Universe. For
many people seeing that picture marked a significant shift in their self-
perception. The meaning of what it means to be human within the setting
of our modern Universe gained a transcendent dimension that was not
there before.

- Allow me to separate human *experiences* into three
  groups. Briefly, these three groups categorize experience
  as follows:
    1. Isolation in the present
    2. Connection to the past or future
    3. Transcendence regardless of time

In the first group are activities in the present that have few or no
implications beyond the doing. I include in this group sleeping, eating,
and walking. The second group of experiences is more complex because
the particulars involve a contrast or tension between the present and the
past or future. In this group I include anger, guilt, shame, sin, success and
failure, joy, contentment, loneliness, fulfillment, confusion being lost.

These experiences in the initial two groups are not complete or exhaustive, but I hope are suggestive enough.

What each of the experiences in the second group has in common is a feeling (tone) that expresses the value and meaning of the experience. This meaning is dependent upon a context of knowing that is larger than the present moment. Having, reflecting on, and learning from these experiences may teach us about transcendence. Maybe there is a subcategory of connective experience that involves a tension between what is and what one thinks should or ought to be. These experiences follow from being informed by a vision of perfection and knowing what is not. They may sharpen our apprehension of the tension between present conditions and some other vision of what might be, but follow from previous knowledge. Also, personal *should and ought* statements have a way of being confused with what one *wants or desires*. A sense of transcendence is involved in values derived from should or ought.

The third group of experiences in my categories depends upon a sense of transcendence for their existence. Without the use of reverence these experiences are impossible. In this group I include thankfulness, forgiving, freedom, feeling oppressed or not free, and accepting helplessness when confronted with the unacceptable. There are others in this group, but these should illustrate my point. All of these experiences have in common that they involve the choices an individual may make in response to living. The choice is in turn dependent upon feeling a contrast or difference. This sense of contrast becomes the basis of choice, the freedom to choose. The choice made will depend upon the sense of transcendent perspective and proportion (reverence) which the individual brings to the moment of decision.

- *Language* enables human beings to name entities, identify relationships, and express feelings and ideas, concepts and desires. Language allows us to distinguish and to abstract, to be concrete and specific as well as general and inclusive. Without language we cannot think. We can act, but not think. Without words to name our thoughts, we humans are oblivious to what is around us and in us. Language enables us to know and express our reverence and our reason. Language is the path that leads to knowing subjects and objects, self and emotions, self and body function, control and power of self in the world. Language allows us to know that apples are fruit and plants are living organisms. Using language is the door to knowing transcendence and responding to life with reverence.

Unless we separate our human capacity for being realistic from our need to be rational, we lose the ability to freely know our emotions and to separate illusion from reality. There is no noun in English to refer to our capacity to be realistic. I cannot write: Our human health depends on our appropriate use of reason, reverence, and _____. Some may suggest that realism is an appropriate noun to fill this blank, but it does not name an active individual capacity. Instead it names a scholastic doctrine or school of thought opposed to idealism. The lack of an appropriate word for our human capacity to be realistic makes my point that the distinction I am suggesting is important, much neglected, and needed.

Over the last few decades our culture has neglected human reverence and its central role in contributing to health. Only by separating reverence and reason may we learn to use reverence and restore the balance between vital human ways of relating to the self, the world, and the creativity of our Universe.

Without language we human beings are locked in the present, the concrete, a very small self. All but the simplest memories are dependent on language. All creative imagining depends on language. For example, unless the English words of theology are given broader meanings, only an increasingly small group of Christians will be able to comfortably, and with benefit, discuss religious concerns.

Human integrity connects words and meanings with events and entities. An individual has integrity when the words they speak and the meanings they intend are congruent with actions and events. The words English supplies us with to talk about matters religious no longer enable us to connect the events of our living to meaning that sustains spiritual health. Many of us can not explore the issues or in some cases even name the issues we need to reflect upon. We are losing our capacity for reverence because we do not have the vocabulary to express our religious ideas and concerns. The great religious traditions of human experience cannot talk with each other because when theological ideas are expressed in English, they come out sounding Christian. There is a bias toward Christianity in English which is rendering the language useless for an increasing proportion of the American-European population. I suspect that there is a similar bias in other languages in other cultures toward the religion that has been dominant over the last 500 to 1,000 years.

How our culture teaches this generation and those to follow to be realistic, use reason and reverence, and stay relevant to self, their human community, the transcendence of humanity, and our precious beautiful organic world is the challenge facing us. This is an epistemological problem because it involves how we know, what we know, and what we hold as important to know.

In our secular culture I see only one tradition and institution which has as its purpose to maintain a balance between our use of reason and our use of reverence— religion. Therefore, I conclude that the practice of religion is so important that it is necessary to broaden the meanings of all theological words in English so that Christianity is an example, not the only referent. There are other ways to be religious. Persons of different religious persuasions need to be able to visit with each other and discuss spiritual concerns without non-Christians being at a disadvantage.

I fear and anticipate that this proposal will be considered creative, ambitious, and controversial. So be it. Each of these three judgments is a path into the transcendent. To follow any of these paths will increase one's capacity for reverence and reasoning. That will be a gift to anyone who seriously becomes engaged.

Chapter 13

The Four Faiths

As I look back over a full career in ministry with Unitarian Universalist congregations, I realize that many of the congregations I have served saw themselves in a humanist tradition. That is to say, the reputation of the minister I have followed has been humanist. I have preached openness to individual freedom of religious belief during most of these years, and welcomed people who need a religious community that allows and encourages them to be themselves within our secular culture. At some point in their lives, most had attended one or several Christian churches and found that their personal integrity would not allow them to continue. Frequently this choice resulted in the individual moving away from family members who did not understand why their son, brother, sister, daughter, grandchild, etc., could not participate in the family's traditional religious practice. The cost of honoring one's religious integrity in terms of family relationships has been high for many of these individuals.

Values and Integrity

These disaffected, yet religious, people believe that when human beings belong to a church as formal members, they should believe what the church teaches about the meaning of life. Having found that they could not say all of the words of the creeds and could not sing some of the hymns, they also found themselves either silently fighting with the sermons or not understanding them. At worst, they believed those sermons were irrelevant, but they kept trying to find a church home where they fit in.

They came looking for a religious community that would allow and enable them to be comfortable with their integrity. They came to the Unitarian Universalist Church looking for a worship service in which they could participate without compromising their integrity. For these people, the connection of words and actions, words and meanings, is extremely important. They need to be in a community of people who are like them. They need to know they are not the only ones who have reached conclusions that preclude attending a traditional Christian church.

I have come to know this experience as a crisis of integrity on Sunday morning. I believe more people than is obvious experience this crisis. I have talked to enough Christian ministers and other Christians who know of this crisis but have not felt compelled to act on it to support this conclusion. Also, the declining number of members in many Christian churches suggests that something significant is wrong or not working. I suggest the question of integrity is one of the major contributing factors.

Anyway, I spent many years ministering to these "come outers" who tended to know what they did not believe. They carried scars and open emotional and intellectual sore points concerning issues of faith expressed in theological language. Many participated and studied in depth their religions of origin; they knew exactly what the words and rituals meant in the tradition they came from. This knowledge caused them so much guilt and grief, they needed a lot of healing. The task I faced was how to help them heal. How could I enable them to say and know what they believed just then? How could they put into symbols the meaning of their living? This was difficult because all theological words in the dictionary are given meanings in terms of Christian content that violated and continues to violate their integrity.

I believe this crisis of religious integrity is one major source behind the crisis of integrity in the politics and business of secular culture. Many people find their integrity violated in religious settings. Religion is so central to setting their values and expectations for living that maintaining integrity in the rest of life has lost importance. Personal integrity has to do with the connection between the words and symbols we use to express our understanding of reality and the meaning of living. We speak and act with integrity when we say what we mean, mean what we say, and shape the activity and events of our living by the values we affirm in our words.

In our society the institutions whose primary task is to give living meaning are religious communities. Large numbers of individuals who live in our secular culture have learned from experience in religious communities that personal and community integrity are not important. While they heard a message of love, they experienced messages of exclusion, fear, hate, and guilt. They found no application of church dogma in the world outside of church. They learned that hard questions arising from doubt are not welcome and are suppressed instead. Some religious leaders will admit their doubts in private but not in public. All of these experiences suggest a crisis of integrity at the heart of Christianity. I believe that the crisis of integrity in religion has infected and is infecting every aspect of our society.

Faiths in a Secular Society

How does anyone conceive or think of an idea when there are no words to express it? Challenging the authority of the dictionary takes self-confidence; where does the ability to gain this strength come from? In response to this challenge, two basic understandings gradually emerged for me. On one hand, I listened to all the voices around me; on the other, I felt there must be a way to respond to them with respect and understanding.

It was crystal clear to me that these people were deeply embedded in secular culture. They knew that Christianity in its popular form did not meet their religious needs. They knew what they did not believe, but did not know what they did believe. Because I wanted to enable people who are immersed in secular culture to realize, know, and say what they do believe, I began searching for ways to put into words the faith that was implicitly sustaining them. Gradually I realized by the way language was being used that I was hearing four different faiths expressed. This was and is an empirical observation for me. The four faiths were humanism, naturalism, mysticism, and theism. Each is adequate and applicable in our secular world. Each has its own coherence and consistency, is adequate and applicable in its own way, and uses a sense of transcendent perspective and proportion.

At the same time I was hearing these four voices, I was searching for a way to understand and relate to each of the four. Was there some overarching way to describe all four and every option within each? The answer I reached involved creating a set of functional definitions for words needed to express religious ideas. Meanings of these words point to our human need to respond to certain experiences without necessarily implying Christian content. For example, religion should enable individuals to do something useful and meaningful with their solitariness by teaching and celebrating how they are connected to relevant transcending reference systems. The idea is that religion's task is to define and enrich how we humans relate to that which transcends us. Meaning in our lives comes from the relationships we know and honor within the *transcendent reference systems of meaning* that surround us. Whitehead does not use this phrase, but his three entities—self, community, God—do suggest how humans know and integrate them when they do something with their solitariness.

Since I was seeking to serve people living in secular culture and practicing religion within a congregation with a humanist tradition, the word *God* was a turn off to them. So I asked what the transcendent reality is that humanists experience, that all human beings experience? The answer was the creativity of the Universe.

Recall that Whitehead suggests that change is the only constant and pervasive element in our lives. Change is creativity at work. Upon reflection I concluded that reflection upon the creativity of our Universe is the path that leads to knowing transcendence and may lead one to know God. Creativity is with every human being during every minute of life. It is immanent as we grow and age, live and die. To acknowledge and accept this reality is to be drawn out into that which is larger than the self, to be drawn out into realms of transcendence.

Reflecting upon this ever-changing transcendent reality of living is one way of seeking to know the meaning and value of one's place and being. It is coming to know that death and time-passing are real and are happening to me. Every human comes to know this reality as they mature. In America most people face it sometime around their 30th birthday or when the first person that is close to them dies. This is a time of theological dis-ease because any resolution depends upon a new understanding of the relationship between the person and that which transcends them. They must work out a new relationship with the transcendent creation and creativity of our Universe.

I came to speak of systems of transcendent meaning (or reference) during the crucible of serving as pastor to people in crisis. When a family member died, the transcendent pattern of family was broken. When a job was lost, the pattern of meaning derived from that activity was no longer operable. When a storm destroyed a home, the geographical place upon which the meaning of living depended was gone. When a person or family moved, they needed to seek out and rebuild a network of friends. Each of these experiences and many more illustrate how we human beings maintain the meaning of our lives by relating to systems of transcendent reference. Each system is a pattern of relatedness.

I also realized that each of the four faiths uses a different transcendent reference system of meaning. Each reaches out from the self and anchors the web of the meaning of their living in a different way. Each is rational, consistent, and coherent within the relevant reality they know and use. Each asks questions until, "It is enough," and then they stop. The stopping points are matters of comfort for the individual, based on experience and the interpretation given to reality.

- *Humanists* draw the meaning of living from within our human community. They believe that all knowledge and values come from this source. They tend to be city folk. They know we get food, energy, shelter, and clothing from our interaction with the world, but these facts are of secondary importance. Most humanists tend to believe that human death is the end of human life, although some humanists believe in life after death and reincarnation. Humanists believe in evolution and understand human living as a genetic link in this transcendent process.

Humanists seek control of things and events. Living in a city tends to lead them to think they are in control, flipping a switch for heat or cool air. Grocery stores provide whatever they want in the way of food. They tend to understand change as a sequence of cause and effect, with a little luck or serendipity happening every now and again. Humanists are concerned about making this world a better place to live in and act as if the value of life comes from what they do today. Many humanists are deeply concerned with issues of justice and injustice in human society, and have great confidence in themselves and other human beings to make this world a better place for all living organisms. When asked what the primary source of their values for governing living is, the human community is the answer they give.

- *Naturalists* have a profound sense that humans are dependent upon and involved with the natural world of living and non-living entities. Our relationship to and dependence upon this transcendent reality is the ultimate source of values and meaning in our human living. Both humanist and naturalist depend upon science as the primary source informing them about the reality in which they live. The sense of dependence upon other living organisms and the overall health of our world puts a limit upon the need for control that naturalists have. They seek knowledge and appropriate acceptance within this transcendent reality.

Evolution is a central way of understanding time and change for naturalists. A larger percentage of naturalists believe in life after death or reincarnation than do humanists, but most believe in death as the end of life. This is consistent with their understanding that human beings are animals, governed by the same laws. Naturalists understand and accept the knowledge gleaned from the ecology movement. They deal with power and control issues, trust and dependence issues, very differently than humanists.

- *Mystics* are people who have experienced a "union with the transcendent creativity of our Universe." This is only one way to say it. Mystics know that science has great power to deal with the material world and that there is more to our world than science is currently able to handle. What the mystics experience is natural to them, rather than supernatural. It may be outside the capabilities of humanists to understand, but it is a result of who they are and what they are capable of experiencing and knowing. Mystics have a profound sense of dependence upon and trust of the transcendent. Many mystics believe in some form of life after death or reincarnation, however, some believe in death as final.

Mystics live in two realms—the material and the spiritual. The world of spirit is one of energy, process, and relationships which are, in some sense, outside of secular culture. This guiding transcendent reference system is too real to be denied, yet it is a little fuzzy to describe precisely. Nevertheless, it informs and shapes mystics' understanding of their living.

- *Theists* know God as a real presence in their living. For some, God is like a river's current that carries you downstream; for others, God is all the abstractions which philosophers and theologians have ascribed to Him over the centuries. God is the ultimate transcendent reference system upon which life depends for order and purpose. Theists tend to believe in some form of life after death.

I have chosen Theism over other god-affirming options because I do not know of any historical limiting reference. This faith may have the most developed and widest variety of any of the four because most traditional religions have been theist. God for theists is the creator of our Universe or, in traditional language, the heavens and the Earth. God sustains order and defines the good in human living. The purpose of life is to be in right relation with God. This is done by faith and reflected in the way one lives one's life. All values come from God.

The functional language presented in the previous chapters of this book were developed to enable me to minister to all four faiths and to challenge each to deepen and enrich their understanding of *the transcendent reference systems of meaning* within which all of us live. The Enough Principle allowed me to accept the validity and goodness of each. Using functional language within each area of theology, I was able to ask central questions of each person and faith, and accept that each person's faith is grounded in experience. The most appreciated part of my ministry was my effort to really listen to their responses. As a pastor, I was empowered to name the different faiths and to know the limits and problems of each. I learned my own identity within the four faiths and how to set it aside, in order to minister to someone in crisis from within the reality of his or her own faith. In planning worship services, I consciously chose which of the four faiths I would include and, in memorial services, I knew how to be relevant to the deceased and to the family members who used various faiths to respond to death.

The "Four Faiths" Workshop

To test the power of functional theological language and the reality and rationality of the four faiths, I created an adult education course based on the four faiths. It used functional definitions for the words and ideas of theology. This provided the language and gave people permission to deal with the central issues of religion. After testing this hypothesis in seven cities, with 14 groups of people totaling somewhere between 500 and 600 individuals participating in the course, I now accept the four faiths as fact.

The course consists of eight two-hour sessions. A theological question is presented in functional terms during each session and a range of responses to these key theological questions is suggested. The options of response are drawn from the human imagination. For example, the second session deals with soteriology, the questions of salvation. Salvation is defined as how one responds to death so as to go on living with vitality and vibrance. What do you believe happens when you die? There are only three possibilities within our human imagination:

1. Some form of life after death
2. Reincarnation
3. "When you die, you are dead;" human life ends, period

All other responses to death seem to me to be a variation on one of these. In presenting this short list, session after session, I intended to be exhaustive of the possibilities. If someone could add to the list of options presented, I was always willing to add another suggestion, but there have been no additions so far. Then I asked participants to claim which option they hold on faith, own it, and assemble in small groups to share their faith with others of like mind.

This methodology forces people who think they do not know what they believe to acknowledge the choices they really have made. For some, it became the first time they had ever openly discussed these issues. I often suggested that each person already was living as if one of the choices were true and invited everyone to try one on for the evening. If it no longer fit the next morning, then I challenged them to figure out what did instead. After 45 minutes of discussion within these self-selected groups, we gathered together in the original large group to listen to reports of each small group discussion. Questions for understanding and clarification were allowed, but not questions of challenge. The idea was to encourage a new understanding of theological faith diversity to emerge so that it can be accepted as real and present. This process will teach something important. To know what your faith is, in positive terms, powerfully aids your ability to maintain spiritual health.

In each city the number of individuals selecting each faith was different. I suspect that the history of the congregations I was serving predisposed the distribution that happened. The result of leading the Four Faiths course so many times is that I am confident the Four Faiths model has the power to respond to the crisis of religious integrity within our secular society.

Chapter 14

The Path of Reverence

I have by now had several months to reflect about the ideas I wrote about in the previous chapters of this book. As the ideas have settled into familiarity, several insights have occurred to me that are surprising and exciting in their newness. Several of them involve paradox and others involve the consequences of placing reason and reverence in tension with each other. Let me conclude by setting forth these reflections. I will first very briefly summarize the basic understandings which inform my conclusions that follow.

Religion is what individuals and communities of individuals do with the fact and experience of individual solitariness. Every individual is religious to the extent that he or she reaches into the transcendent reference systems of self, community, and creativity to establish and know the meaning of living. Meaning for humans has to do with the relationships in which each individual participates. Human relatedness has two dimensions—quantity and quality. Both of these elements have numerous ways they may be understood depending on the culture, ethnic community, religious tradition, and the individual involved in defining meaning. The age of the individual is also a determinative factor in giving definition to significant meaning. As we grow older, the meaning of living that sustains our living changes.

The purpose of any formal religion should be to respond to the issues growing out of individual solitariness. Of all these issues, some affect our living directly, for example, living with the knowledge of death and dying; living with the paradox that cause-and-effect and grace are both aspects of reality; living with the experiences of prediction, power and control, and helplessness.

Paradoxes Unlimited

Is it not a paradox that there are many ways for human beings to be religious, all dealing with the reality that transcends everyone? Most of these ways of religion function well enough. Each is relevant to the lives to which it gives meaning and speaks to a particular cultural setting. Each should claim to deliver meaning that will give vitality and vibrance to living. All claim to carry truth, yet none should claim absolute truth; even so, some do. If time and distance isolate religions, the claim of absolute truth stands unchallenged, but no such isolation is part of contemporary reality and even less will exist in the future.

Acceptance of the relativity of religious truth is crucial for peace within the human community which supports a wide diversity of religious faith and hope. There is no single absolutely correct or best way to be religiously human. Instead, many ways present themselves. Every individual needs to know and participate in the way that is supportive of his or her life. It is truly a paradox. Every person needs to act as if his or her way is the only way and yet remain open to accept all the other ways of being religious that support the health, faith, and hope of other human beings. Living with this paradox seems to me to depend upon a sense of transcendent perspective and proportion (reverence). This sense allows any person not to be threatened by difference, and to live with the commitment that sustains their living.

The conditions of relativity must haunt every effort to be realistic, rational, and reverent. Although there is no absolute best for all people, a specific point of reference or vantage point exists from which every individual knows, lives, and must be committed in faith and hope. All individuals live their lives as if some pattern of transcendent reference gives satisfactory meaning to their living. Most people are more comfortable if they are part of a community of people who know and celebrate this pattern. However, many people unconsciously use a pattern of transcendent meaning.

Living is a series of choices and commitments. To refuse to choose is a choice. There is a sense in which some religious meaning informs, either implicitly or explicitly, every choice of every individual.

Transcendence means larger than. A conclusion from using this understanding and perception is an existing correlation between goodness and larger than. The implication is that a more inclusive perspective is better. This is not always so. Every individual and religion has the power to invoke the *Enough Principle* when it seems appropriate to put it in tension with their sense of transcendence. However, if you are functioning within a fully developed religious perspective, usually little or no tension is present. If one is reflecting on the difference between two or more individual levels of understanding, more tension occurs. If one is comparing different religions, different ways of knowing transcendence will surface, as will how and when the Enough Principle is used. Every person, community, and religion lives with the consequences of when they have accepted, "*It is enough.*" And every person, community, and religion lives with the meaning they have constructed from the transcendent reference systems of meaning.

Reasoning in terms of consistent and coherent thinking and action is good as long as it is governed by a sense of when, "It is enough." Reasoning without a sense of enough will always lead to the absurd or a striving for an impossible or demonic state of perfection. Most people come to know a good and proceed to move toward it with consistency. However, almost every good in life becomes bad, or just boring, when overdone or one gets too much of it. You have to know when, "It is enough."

Good is a process, not a state frozen in time or some future condition of imagined perfection. All reasoning takes place within a perspective of reality. Reasoning many times is toward a known goal or to solve a problem. Most human reasoning is guided by accepted rules of process, such as, logic or relational values. It is a paradox that reasoning is what we humans do very well, yet reasoning is dependent on the conceptual reality within which one is operating. Human success in reasoning may very well depend on whether the reasoning is adequately and appropriately informed by reverence.

Living with a strong and working sense of transcendent perspectives may cause some discomfort or anxiety in the short term. When two people have different abilities to know and respond to transcendence, there will be tension between them. When a person comes into a group and brings a new or different perception of transcendence, the group must accommodate in some way. Either the individual lets go and accepts the group way of being or, if the individual acts as a change agent, the individual's vision may challenge the community to change. Many times an individual joins a community because the tradition of the community challenges the individual to grow and enlarge his or her religious perspective.

I believe that we humans will function throughout our lives more effectively if we separate our capacity to be rational and our ability to respond with reverence. We need both capacities working together to sustain health of self and community. In any given situation a person needs to be appropriately rational and reverent. Since this distinction has not been given much attention in recent years, I urge that reverence be taught explicitly to all children and also to all adults who have neglected it in the process of reaching maturity. A sense of reverence begins by learning that the family and my in-group are larger than my ego. Learning how my in-group fits into the larger human community and how our human community is dependent upon the world of nature is crucial to developing a sense of reverence. Reverence begins with gaining a transcendent perspective and then gaining a sense of proportion between the multiplicity of values emerging from knowing that every concrete moment is embedded in one or more transcendent contexts.

As my sense of reverence became conscious and active, I realized that paradox permeates human living. **Paradox** is the recognition that two rather contradictory perceptions are true of the same thing or situation simultaneously. Perceiving paradox depends on understanding that transcendence is an enveloping reality of every moment of living. Paradox is a far more important category of understanding than our secular culture has acknowledged. Let me list a few that are essential to every moment of human living:

- Every person is both a subject and object every moment of life.
- Every entity is both a subject and object every moment.
- All entities are both facts and a process of change all the time.
- All entities of our world are both discrete objects and a pattern of relationships.
- The reality in which humans live is governed by cause-and-effect and grace all the time.
- Change in our lives is predictable and not predictable.
- Every value is both good and bad.
- More is good and too much is not good.
- Ownership is good, yet possessiveness is not.
- Freedom is good, yet too much will be destructive to any individual. Individual freedom depends on community and knowing and accepting appropriate limits.
- Perfection is a good ideal yet, when followed rigorously, leads to the demonic.
- Individuals and communities must coexist. They are mutually dependent, yet the needs of each, in many cases, are seen as opposed to one another.
- A room may be in great need of cleaning and decorating, yet be well used, much loved, and very comfortable.

- Individuals express their individuality by using peer group values.
- Every religion is both concrete and abstract.
- Every religion is both functional and filled with content, history, and tradition.
- Humans may be both rational and reverent.
- There is one inclusive reality, yet there are many perspectives from which our human values and lives are drawn.

Increasing our human perception and acceptance of transcendence will increase our sense of relativity and paradox. As our human sense of paradox increases, our individual freedom will increase. This is so because, if one is in the middle of a paradox, one may choose how to balance the tension between the values involved. If one sees only one set of values, no choice is possible.

Humor, paradox, and a sense of transcendence are intimately related. A person who is concerned only with facts will tend to lack a sense of humor. Laughing at oneself and with others depends on seeing a transcendent perspective of a situation that is rather serious and or concrete. Most jokes are understood and evoke laughter only if one perceives more than one implication to a set of facts or the way something is said. If you do not get a joke, it is because you do not perceive how two or more meanings are suggested by one set of words, a picture, or action.

Reason and Reverence

Racism is rational. Racial prejudice is based on a consistent application of an in-group's values. If one stays within a coherent and consistent application of the values of an in-group, whether defined by skin color, race, religion, or economic class, one will act from an "-ism" based on that in-group. Prejudice will break down only with experiences that show these values to be inadequate, inapplicable, or incoherent. Experiences enable us to know the world from a larger perspective, a vantage point that will dissolve the hate and fear of racism. Teaching transcendent perspective and proportion (reverence) is the key to healing our world that is so divided by tribal, racial, and in-group tensions.

The ability to forgive self or another human being follows from reverence, not from reason. Consistency is so central to reason that maintaining individual and in-group integrity and honor are the guiding values that follow from it. Mistakes, failures, insults—all pose a threat to one's integrity and honor, to one's sense of self as perfect and the center of concern. Reason tells us to drive for perfection, never to accept failure, and to seek revenge for insults. Only some sense of transcendent perspective will lead us to act upon a sense of, "It is enough." Only a sense of perspective that is larger than the present moment will enable forgiving oneself for not being perfect, for not winning every race, for failing to reach some goal. Only a transcendent perspective of self will enable forgiveness for an insult given by another. A person can maintain his or her sense of self-worth when insulted only if a transcendent perspective of self as good enough prevails. To forgive another is to accept that the other has a strong emotion or problem that is not yours. This act of forgiveness depends upon a sense of proportion that includes self, the other person, and the larger context within which both live.

The capacity to be thankful also follows from reverence, not reason. Reason leads one to conclude that individuals have rights, that work deserves reward, and that goodness in my life is my just desserts. Only when we begin to ask, "Why are things this way and not some other?" may we be led to a feeling of thanksgiving. Only as we contrast the good and the not so good, the amount of goodness I have in contrast to the goodness you have, may we begin to suspect that rights and rewards are not ours by virtue of being an American and working hard. Both these reflections involve transcendent perspective. And a healthy resolution to the anxiety created by these perspectives will necessitate a sense of proportion based on a transcendent perspective of self. Thankfulness follows from the use of reverence.

Let me conclude by saying that I believe human health depends on a balanced and appropriately realistic use of both reason and reverence. A variety of ability to use these three mental faculties will occur within any human community. Let us honor and benefit from this variety. Let us appreciate the paradox that any one person may be very intelligent and still not have the capacity to know what some other person knows from direct experience. Let each of us be given the time, space, and support needed for us to achieve vitality and vibrance in our living as we do what we need to do with our solitariness. May the blessing of realism, reason, and reverence enable us to create and sustain a world in which every individual finds spiritual health in a religion that is grounded in his or her own culture.

Glossary

Functional Definitions of Theological Words and Concepts

Adequate–Inclusion of all the elements or items necessary for complete understanding. In religion adequacy is achieved when individuals are enabled to accept, understand, and give meaning to all the events of living between birth and death, and to place living within a transcendent context. None of the many questions arising from reflection on the way every individual participates in the transcendent patterns that surround living may be left without a response.

Applicability–Deals with what degree of success or productivity ideas, understandings,and faith work in the real world. How well do abstract ideas function in concrete living?

Christology–The study of how religions use symbols.

Creativity of the Universe–In this essay, the constant change that is part ofmoment and duration of time. Creativity has two aspects: one moving toward complexity and one moving toward simplicity. We humans know this creativity as we grow, age, move. Living for all organisms is dependent upon both aspects of creativity. It is a paradox that both aspects of creativity may be good or bad depending on who benefits from the change.

Coherence–All the needed pieces are present and fit together.

Consistent–Without contradiction, but does not exclude paradox.

Enough Principle–All humans have at some times a sense of when enough is enough. When we evoke this feeling, we stop what we are doing. I find that this sense of enough is central to civilized society, to every individual's spiritual health. To give the feeling more status I raise it to the level of a principle. Reason as consistency drives us to seek perfection and extremes. Invoking the Enough Principle enables us to live with ourselves and within reality. Knowing when to stop or let go is important to human spiritual health.

Epistemology–The study of how we gain religious knowledge.

Eschatology–The study of last things, involving time and change.

Ethics–The study of our human use of values, *that is* anything or entity toward which a human being will or has expended effort, time, or wealth.

Faith–That which enables human beings to live with and through despair, depression, loss, illness, grief, dying, and death with trust, knowing risk, dependence. That which enables human being to respond to living with "IN SPITE OF . . . I WILL BE COMMITTED." The matrix of relationships that establishes the meaning of living and brings spiritual health to individuals as they do something with their solitariness. The beliefs, values, and understandings to which an individual or community of individuals are committed that bring order and organization to living. Faith involves how individuals relate to that which transcends them.

Four Faiths model–Humanism, naturalism, mysticism, and theism state in positive terms what some individuals in secular society believe is the meaning of life. Each is based on undeniable personal experience of individuals. Each has a different perspective of reality that serves as the definitive transcendent reference system for its values, rational activity, and reverence. Each uses the English language slightly differently. There are several options within each of the major four faiths. Many people experience some of the boundaries between the four as fuzzy.

Functional definitions–The meaning of words given in terms based on experience, instead of the content of one religion.

Grace–The exquisite timing of events in our lives.

Humanism–Use of the human community as the primary transcendent reference system of meaning to describe the religious content of just one of four faiths appropriate for a secular society.

In-group–A group of people defined by values held in common; for example, a family, a tribe, a nation, followers of a religion.

Integrity–Refers to the relationship between human experience and the words used to describe that experience. People have integrity when their words communicate a congruence with their experience and the experience of other people, that is, they say what they mean and do what they say, and their words describe reality as others remember it and experience it.

Irrational–Thinking or behavior which involves one or more contradictions of values.

Liturgy–Structure of a worship service. The way the elements of a service are put together to create the dance or drama of meaning that is significant for the participating religious community.

Meaning–The relationships human beings have and honor with their transcending reference systems of reality. Relatedness has two dimensions, quantity and quality. When either or both increase, an individual will experience an increase in meaning.

Metaphysics–The study of what is real, and why it is real. How human beings respond to the reality they live in and believe to surround them. Reality for every human being is composed of physical things, relationships, ideas, values, and other people and living organisms, etc. Individuals differ in their capacity to discern, to know, to integrate, and to interact with the elements of reality. Therefore, human beings respond in many ways to the reality in which they are embedded.

Moral values–A set of values which a person or community expects to be applied or followed with consistency.

Mysticism—The faith of human beings who experience a "union with the transcendent." In secular culture, mystics know that the sciences do not deal with this kind of experience which is so strong or occurs frequently enough that it cannot be denied.

Mystics—People who draw the meaning of life and the values that shape their living from the experience of their relationship in union with the transcendent that they come to know in their solitariness.

Myth—Stories carrying meaning and understanding about human living. Myths are to religion as theories are to science. Both set forth relationships of concern and interest.

Naturalism—One of the four faiths which understands human living as participating in and dependent upon the natural world as the transcendent reference system of meaning. Naturalists draw all their values from and find their religious identity within this system.

Non-rational—Those elements of an individual's world that are neither rational nor irrational: for example, facts, rocks, chairs, feelings, faith, objects, ideas, emotions.

Ontology—The study of being, doing and power. In functional theology, ontology asks these questions: To what extent are humans in control of their living? To what extent are they not in control? Does cause and effect or the exquisite timing of grace dominate our living? Who or what is in charge of our lives?

Perspective—Knowledge of how individuals are dependent on and embedded in layers or webs of transcendence. Religions use perspectives of transcendence to enhance and nourish human spiritual health.

Proportion—The sense and wisdom that maintains the tension and balance between competing perspectives of transcendence, and the values derived from them within the living of individuals.

Rational—Thinking consistently and coherently, without contradiction, within an accepted reality or set of values. This does not exclude paradox.

Realistic–To be adequate and applicable.

Reality–The creation and creativity in which human beings live. The matrix of facts and relationships which go to make up our cosmic epoch, our Universe. Every individual creates meaning from and relates to only a portion of the final inclusive reality. Every religious faith gives an interpretation to some portion of the final inclusive reality.

Reason–The human capacity to be consistent and coherent.

Relativity–With regards to religion and truth, says that no religious faith or truth is absolute or universally true for all ethnic groups of humans. Each religious faith carries truth and meaning for its cultural setting and its followers. As a religion's cultural setting changes so must its way of providing meaning also change. Every individual lives as if some transcendent web of meaning is real and true. However, the cultural setting in which a religion seeks to deliver spiritual health for individuals will determine the degree of vitality and vibrance any given religion achieves. Every individual lives as if some religious faith is appropriate and applicable to their living.

Religion–What individuals and communities do with the fact of individual solitariness. The religious response to solitariness deepens and enriches our human knowledge of self, how we need and are involved in community, and are embedded in the creation and creativity of our Universe. Religion is how human beings live within that which transcends them.

Reverence–Begins with a sense of transcendent perspective and proportion. In essence it is knowing which transcendent reference systems of meaning are relevant and appropriate to any given situation and being able to appropriately balance the competing values in the situation. Using reverence to respond to solitariness leads to religion. Reverence deepens and enriches our knowledge of self, and how we need and are involved in community, and are embedded in the creation and creativity of our universe. Religion uses reverence to give us acceptance and understanding of change through which we may know the creativity of the Universe and or God.

Ritual –An repeated action which is understood to be real, in and of itself, that reminds us of meaning and connection through its symbolic aspect of one or more layers.

Salvation–Concerns how human beings resolve the knowledge of dying and death so as to live with spiritual health and affirmation. One is saved if one has a faith that brings acceptance of death, the capacity for reverence, and vitality to living.

Saved–A state of knowing you have resolved to live with the knowledge that death is a part of living and will be the end of your life on Earth.

Sin–Missing the mark that is the goodness of living.

Solitariness–Points to the fact that every individual human lives his or her life once, and no one can do it for anyone else. Friends and companions may be with you, but you suffer the trials and tribulations, the joys and jubilation of your own living.

Soteriology–The study of salvation. How human beings live with the knowledge of death.

Spiritual health–The way the web of meaning surrounds every individual to sustain his or her vitality and vibrance of living. Spiritual health concerns how the transcendent reference systems of meaning are known, accepted, and integrated into an organic whole which is realistic, relevant, rational, and reverent of the creation and creativity within which the individual lives.

Theism–One of the four faiths in which human beings have experience of a presence known as a "THOU." They name this presence God. Looking at any theist tradition which has served to bring meaning to human living over many generations, one will find layers and layers of meaning and interpretation of the being or concept of God. Each generation has added to what the previous ones have revealed. God for theists points to a transcendent flowing pattern of events that the individual trusts and knows his or her profound dependence upon. The dependence and trust are known from direct experience.

Theology–Human reflection using memory and imagination about how individuals and communities of individuals relate to the transcending and transcendent reference systems of meaning within which living takes place. The purpose of theology is to establish, maintain, and celebrate order, meaning, and purpose in human living. As theology tells us what individuals have done and are doing with their solitariness, it is the verbal side of what individuals do with their solitariness (religion).

Transcendence, transcendent–Larger than.

Transcendent reference systems of meaning–Those patterns of things, entities, actions, and relationships that are larger than the self and are used to give connection and relatedness to the living of an individual alone and in assembled communities. Those patterns of things and relationships used to sustain spiritual health for individuals. Individuals find these patterns through religion as well as secular activities.

Values–Anything or entity toward which a human being will expend or has expended effort, time, or wealth. Moral values are those sets of values which a person or community expect to be applied or followed with consistency.

Worship–A symbolic drama of an event or relationship and its meaning for human living within the transcendent context that surrounds individual solitariness.

About the Author

Fred Campbell developed his ability to see and hear, read and understand, wonder and reflect, as he earned a B.A. in Philosophy at Earlham College. Four years in the U.S. Navy as a junior officer taught him the differences between honesty and deception, reality and appearance, and a great deal about power and authority, order and discipline, conformity and commitment. While earning a B.D. degree at Meadville Theological School of Lombard College in Chicago, he studied Christian faith and history, small group dynamics and process, and the liberal religious tradition as expressed in Unitarian Universalism.

The Rev. Fred F. Campbell went to Arkansas and served as a liberal minister in Little Rock. There and in the churches he served over the next 15 years, he grappled with the challenges of religious faith in secular society, that is, how caring and loving people meet and live through their experiences of birth and illness, grief and death, doubt and trust, despair and hope. He learned that theology gains its value as it delivers pragmatic faith and hope to carry people through the day-to-day routine of living which is sometimes filled with crises. Gradually he came to realize that he was seeing and hearing four ways of expressing faith. Each was drawing values and meaning from a different source. All the sources were transcendent of the self. In seeking to meet each person's spiritual needs, Rev. Campbell was forced to push religious words beyond Christian meanings to their experiential base. His conversations with congregants during this process allowed a set of functional meanings to emerge that enabled each of these four faiths to be expressed positively. Acceptance of dual realities—these diverse faiths and the power of each one— resulted from these new understandings.

Moving to six cities in six different states as an interim UU minister provided an opportunity to test the applicability of the Four Faiths model. Did functional religious language have the power to express the religious needs and concerns of people living in different regions? From numerous observations across the U.S., Rev. Campbell is confident that functional religious language helps people embedded in secular culture open themselves to religious concerns. It then provides them a means, first, to deepen and enrich their faith, hope, and spiritual living; and second, to use non-prejudiced language in conversation with followers of major world religions.

Four Faiths:

An Adult Religious Education Course in Eight Sessions

by Rev. Fred F. Campbell

Explore

Functional Concepts of Theology

within

Humanism Naturalism Mysticism Theism

through conversations with other workshop participants.

Each two-hour session presents religious ideas and concerns which persist within our secular society, followed by small group discussions and shared reports to the larger group. An acceptance of diverse faiths usually results for the participants in this course.

This **(43-page)** curriculum guide describes the structure and flow of each session. It also includes an outline of the ideas presented during each session.

To Order This Course Guide, 1999 edition,

send $12.00 for text, shipping, and handling to:

Rev. Fred F. Campbell

1186 Wild Cherry

Willianston, MI 48895

TO ARRANGE ON-SITE LEADERSHIP,

contact the author by

email Fredffc@aol.com